Plant Manager's R   Quality Assurance i
Reference Handbook of Quality in Manufacturing

3 Books in 1

Louis Bevoc and Allison Shearsett

Published by
NutriNiche System LLC

Louis Bevoc books...simple explanations of complex subjects

Plant Manager's Reference Handbook

12 Essential Skills and Why They are Needed

Louis Bevoc

Published by
NutriNiche System LLC

Louis Bevoc books...simple explanations of complex subjects

Introduction	4
Scope	4
Skills	5
Delegation	5
Organization	7
Recruitment	15
Motivation	16
Communication	20
Strategic	24
Training	29
Decision making	32
Emotional intelligence	35
Problem solving	40
Sales	44
Political	45
Summary	49

Introduction

One person is largely responsible for everything that happens in a manufacturing facility. This individual oversees every aspect of the operation by breaking down complicated problems and projects into manageable tasks that can be delegated to lower level supervisors. This individual is involved in some capacity with every employee and every department, and he or she is known as the plant manager.

Plant managers are actively involved in daily operations and long-term plans of manufacturing facilities. Some of their more important duties include overseeing production, maintenance, engineering, safety, quality, shipping, receiving, inventory control, and building projects. Along the same lines, they monitor budgets, expenditures, costs, and purchases. In this capacity, plant managers bear responsibility for the implementation, maintenance, and enforcement of all plant related projects, processes, policies, and procedures. They deal with people at all levels, and they are often the most visible employees in their organizations.

Plant managers are often on call 24/7. They are rarely able to leave the facility for extended periods of time and not be contacted for one reason or another. Quite simply, they are so important that some decisions cannot be made without their approval or input. If they cannot be present, then they provide others with instructions on how to proceed with problems or situations.

The information in the above paragraphs is a brief description of the position and responsibilities of a plant manager. This description could be much more detailed, but it is informative enough to progress to the next section that discusses the major focus of this book.

Scope

Anyone familiar with the *Louis Bevoc* series of books understands that they all focus on different aspects of organizations. Certain books deal with specific areas of manufacturing such as quality assurance, research & development, inventory control, warehousing, packaging, industrial/organizational psychology, technology, operations, and human resources. Other books explore cultures, social skills, emotions, risk management, teams, goals, vision, diversity, and leadership. Last, but certainly not least, some books examine the darker side of organizational life including sexual harassment, workplace violence, safety, downsizing, stress, lies, stereotyping, and toxic leadership.

The focus of this book is plant management. More specifically, it is a reference handbook that lists important skills of plant managers and explains why they are needed. These skills include the following:

- Delegation
- Organization
- Recruitment
- Motivation
- Communication
- Strategic
- Training
- Decision making
- Emotional intelligence

- Problem solving
- Sales
- Political

The next section breaks down the skills listed above.

Skills

Before discussing the 12 essential skills, it must be noted that plant managers are expected to have knowledge of the plant processes and procedures that they are overseeing. They need to understand what happens at the production floor level...maybe not as a laborer, but at least as a supervisor or support position. They need some type of experience before attaining the top position...regardless of their level of formal education. Some manufacturers require plant managers to spend days, weeks, or even months in specially designed programs to enhance their chances for success even if they have the necessary credentials to take on the job.

It is now time to move into the crux of this book. Below are 12 essential skills needed for plant managers along with reasons that these skills are needed.

Delegation

Most plant managers need to delegate tasks in order to achieve the goals that have been set by themselves or their organizations. Delegation is essential for plant managers because they cannot accomplish everything they need to do without the help of others. When they delegate, they relieve some of their workload, and this allows them to focus on other tasks. They must assign responsibilities to subordinate employees....or they jeopardize their own jobs due to performance issues.

Plant managers need to understand that productivity increases when work is delegated. This is because that work can be broken down into manageable portions and given to different employees. Psychologically, this is easier on employees than handling an entire project because they are not faced with an overwhelming amount of work that needs to be finished. They see a small of work, and this inspires them to get it done. In this sense, delegation empowers workers because they are given a job and have decision making power. They then take responsibility for the jobs they are performing, and that responsibility commits them to the goals and objectives of the organization.

Delegation is beneficial because it gives employees the opportunity to learn. They are assigned specific tasks, and they are responsible for following those tasks through to completion. This takes time and effort, but it also provides a real-world learning experience that cannot be obtained by reading a book or sitting in a classroom. Smart plant managers understand this education is valuable, and that is one reason why they delegate.

Plant managers also need to understand that manufacturing facilities operate more efficiency when work is delegated because jobs can be matched with employees' skills. This allows for the jobs to be broken down based on expertise. For example, cost aspects can be delegated to accountants, specification aspects can be delegated to quality assurance people, architectural aspects can be delegated to engineers, and training aspects can be delegated to human resources personnel.

When plant managers cannot delegate, they often end up micromanaging. This means they devote major time to minor details and focus intently on aspects of their jobs that they consider important. Unfortunately for their subordinates, this means every detail of their job is scrutinized...which often hinders productivity.

The actions of micromanaging plant managers are not all bad. In fact, their decisions are usually well thought since they are typically capable individuals who understand the needs of the manufacturing facility. However, the downside of their actions is their counter-productivity. Many times their subordinates are perfectly capable of making decisions, but they are not allowed to do so by micromanaging plant managers. This delays tasks from getting completed, hinders organizational efficiency, and prevents goals and objectives from being accomplished.

Plant managers who micromanage also prevent mistakes by making sure their employees adhere to specific details of work-related tasks. However, for the most part, micromanagers hinder productivity be monitoring processes and procedures far too closely. They are sometimes known as "workplace bullies" due to the high level of control that they possess...and their refusal or inability to delegate or relinquish that control.

Based on the above, it is rather obvious delegation is useful in organizations. However, plant managers also need to understand that there are times when they should not delegate work. For example, they should not delegate work simply because it is something that they do not enjoy doing. If plant managers have important tasks that they need to attend to and their plate is full, then they should delegate menial work to their subordinates. However, if they delegate work simply because they do not want to do it, then that is a clear sign of laziness...and plant employees will see this as a weakness.

Plant managers also need to keep their power in check so they do not abuse it. In terms of delegation, this means that they cannot believe their power gives them the right to delegate everything to others. While this might actually be true in some cases, it is not right...and it counteracts many of the benefits of delegation.

One last situation where work should not be delegated is when employees do not have the expertise to handle it. If these individuals are not capable, then they will not get the job done. Plant managers who ignore this rule will end up causing problems for their employees and their facility.

One way that plant managers can avoid delegation problems in their facilities is to follow a few basic guidelines. These guidelines include:

- *Matching expertise*

    It is important to select the right employee for the job. Employees are easily discouraged when they do not have the expertise to handle a task that has been delegated to them. Every plant manager can delegate, but choosing the person with the right skills for the task is much more difficult. In terms of a matching expertise, "failing to plan, means planning to fail."

- *Explaining reasoning*

    Employees need to be made aware of the reason for the delegation. Workers want to know why there are performing a task and what their contribution means...rather than simply being told to do it. When they understand the reasoning, they take ownership of the task, and this increases the chance for success. Plant managers need to understand that employees who do not know why they are doing something feel like mushrooms...they are left alone to grow in the dark!

- *Define responsibilities*

    Employees need to know exactly what is expected of them. Plant managers who fail to define responsibilities do much more damage to their organizations than they realize. Valuable resources are depleted when employees are not sure of their responsibilities. Time, effort, and money are wasted until they understand exactly what is expected of them.

- *Encourage participation*

    Employees need to be involved in the process and asked for their opinions. This motivates them to take action and inspires them to do their best. Plant managers who do not encourage feedback lose out on valuable information that could be provided by the employees doing the work. That information could be used to make the completion of future tasks faster and more efficient.

- *Follow-up*

    Plant managers need to communicate with employees after they have been delegated tasks. Lines of communication should be kept open for questions and comments. Follow up is about being proactive rather than reactive. Plant managers who do not establish a dialog with their employees are not available to answer questions that arise, and the end result is workers getting off track.

- *Provide feedback*

    Plant managers need to let employees know how they performed after their tasks are completed. After all, these employees invested a lot of time and effort, and they deserve to hear about the outcome. Additionally, compliments and constructive criticism help build relationships that assure success with the next delegated task. Plant managers who do not provide feedback are making a mistake because feedback drives the change that is necessary for making improvements in the future.

Organization

Manufacturing facilities need to be organized in order to operate smoothly and run at peak efficiency. Organization starts with leadership, and plant managers are the top leaders in manufacturing facilities. It can be argued that leadership should not be listed under this section (organization) because it is an important part of every skill in this book. However, manufacturing consists of a serious of processes and, without organization; these processes are not effective.

Six basic styles of leadership are listed below. Plant managers can fall into one or more of these styles, and they all require skill in order to be effective.

- *Authoritarian*

    Plant managers of this style want their organizations to be as efficient as possible, and they believe order and structure are the best way to achieve efficiency. Direct supervision is important and subordinates are kept on a tight leash. Policies and procedures are strictly followed, relationships are professional, and communication moves from top to bottom.

    Authoritarian plant managers focus on control. They maintain close supervision so they do not lose control, and they see other types of leadership style (such as democratic) as inefficient because control is limited.

    Advantages and disadvantages of this leadership style are as follows:

    Advantages

    One advantage of an authoritarian leadership style involves orderliness. There is little opportunity for disorder or chaos because strict controls are in place. Things tend to remain in proper order from start to finish, and this eliminates confusion.

    Another advantage of this style involves communication. Since most orders are direct, there is limited room for distorted messages…and miscommunication is less frequent than that experienced with other leadership styles.

    Disadvantages

    Probably the biggest disadvantage to the authoritarian leadership style is it creates a climate of fear. Employees are afraid to argue or question decisions made by authoritarian plant managers because they might be jeopardizing their jobs.

    Another disadvantage is the fact that creativity and diversity are stifled. Employees are not entitled to opinions, and there is no room for debate or disagreement. There is only one right answer…and it comes from the authoritarian plant manager.

- *Democratic*

    Democratic plant managers share decision-making responsibilities with other employees. They believe in debate, and they encourage discussion. This leadership style allows employees to feel good about themselves and the fact that they are involved in decision-making processes. Democratic plant managers view authoritarian leadership as too rigid with no room for new ideas or creativity.

    One important and often overlooked aspect of this style is the fact that democratic plant managers maintain control over the company and the employees within it. They decide who participates in the decision-making, and typically this does not include everyone. Additionally, these plant managers will make decisions without other people's input if necessary. If discussions get off track or suggestions do not make sense, then democratic plant managers will take charge.

    Democratic leadership works well in organizations where workers are skilled and need little direction. It has limited value in manufacturing facilities because employees are often unskilled and in need of direction.

    Advantages and disadvantages of this leadership style are as follows:

    Advantages

    > Democratic leadership motivates people and improves productivity because people get to voice their thoughts and opinions. Solutions to problems are more creative and diverse due to the wide variety of people involved. This style of leadership also encourages constant improvement because employees feed off each other's ideas during discussion.

    Disadvantages

    > The downside of the democratic leadership style is that it is not applicable to every organization. It works well with skilled employees, but not so well with those who lack skills. For example, a manufacturing facility staffed with temporary employees would not be productive under democratic leadership. Employees simply do not know enough about their jobs to work without supervision, and their knowledge is too limited to be involved in decision-making processes.

- *Laissez-faire*

    This leadership style lets employees make all decisions. The "hands-off" approach puts power into the hands of rank and file personnel with very little direction from management.

Plant manager with laissez-fair leadership styles must provide the tools and materials necessary for employees to perform their jobs. Once employees have the necessary resources, these plant managers' roles are reduced to that of mentors. They then need to:

1. Make themselves available if their assistance is required
2. Provide feedback after completion of a job or task

This style of leadership might seem like it would produce a chaotic and confusing work environment. However, this is typically not the case because plant managers are available when needed, and they provide feedback about employee performance. In short, laissez-faire workplaces are the epitome of self-governance.

Advantages and disadvantages of this leadership style are as follows:

Advantages

A laissez-faire plant manager promotes a climate of trust. Workers basically manage themselves, and this creates a two-way trust between the plant manager and employees. Employees are trusted to do their jobs correctly, and they trust the plant manager to let them do whatever is needed to complete tasks. Additionally, employees become better at making the right decisions as they become more experienced, and this further lessens the need for plant management support.

Disadvantages

The biggest disadvantage to this style of management is it will not work in many organizations. For laissez-faire leadership to be effective, all employees need to be educated, skilled, and experienced. This is typically not the case in a manufacturing workplace. Many employees need supervision to complete job tasks because they are not capable of doing everything on their own.

Additionally, this style will not work if plant managers do not provide appropriate feedback. While direct supervision is not necessary, plant managers need to review and comment on jobs after they are completed. Employees who do not receive input might not be working toward achieving organizational goals and objectives.

- *Paternalistic*

Paternalistic plant managers are exactly what the word implies...they act as a parent to the employees. They are more like a father figure than a supervisor because they take charge of their workers' lives inside and outside of work. They show concern by supporting employee ideas, protecting their best interests, encouraging them to give their best effort, and providing rewards for their success. In return, they expect loyalty from their employees...just like parents expect from children.

Advantages and disadvantages of this leadership style are as follows:

Advantages

The biggest advantage of the paternalistic leadership style is it builds self-confidence. Employees work hard due to their loyalty to the organization, and this pays off in terms of goal accomplishment. A feeling of success develops as they move on to their next task, and they build the self-confidence necessary to accomplish other goals. Essentially, a positive cycle results where employees build confidence, attain goals, and help plant managers achieve objectives.

Disadvantages

A major problem with this style of leadership involves workplace favoritism. Plant managers tend to favor the employees who are the most loyal to the organization. Favoritism is not uncommon with other leadership styles, but it is more severe with paternalistic plant managers because loyalty is so important.

- *Transactional*

Transactional plant managers use rewards and punishment to influence employee behavior. They use rewards when performance meets or exceeds expectations, and they use punishment when performance is below expectations. Rewards are typically monetary, material, or psychological...the idea is simply to recognize performance achievements. Punishment usually involves corrective action and a plan for improvement...the idea is to eliminate the problem and progress toward satisfactory performance.

Transactional plant managers believe in rules and standardized practices. They like to develop systems and hold employees accountable for meeting established standards. Unlike other leadership styles, such as democratic, they prefer the status quo and typically do not like change. Efficiency, flow, and productivity rank above everything else...and the best way to maximize these variables is to establish goals and objectives.

Advantages and disadvantages of this leadership style are as follows:

Advantages

One advantage of this type of leadership style is simplicity. Rewards and punishments are easily understood by all employees without training or detailed explanation by the plant manager.

Another advantage involves speed. Rewards are an instantaneous motivator for employees. When used correctly, these rewards can improve workplace morale at crucial times.

Disadvantages

Plant managers must have a constant presence in order for this leadership style to be successful. Success or failure of employees is dependent upon appraisal...and they cannot be appraised if the plant manager is not present. Additionally, when the plant manager is not around, employees might resort to deviant behavior to avoid punishment for not achieving organizational goals.

Another negative of transactional leadership involves rewards. Rewards are powerful motivators that can improve morale in critical periods. However, the increase in morale is only temporary. The positive perception of the reward wears off in a relatively short period of time, and employees can revert to thinking negatively about their jobs, the organization, and the plant manager. In other words, the inspirational effects of rewards are short-term.

- *Transformational*

Transformational plant managers are typically knowledgeable and charismatic. They work tirelessly to get personnel to think independently about what is best for the manufacturer. This is accomplished by setting objectives that drive employees to work harder and increase performance. In short, the goal of this leadership style is to "transform" employee thinking so they want to work toward improving the organization and taking it to the next level.

Advantages and disadvantages of this leadership style are as follows:

Advantages

Transformational plant managers are visionaries because they are able to assess challenging situations and formulate plans for improvement. Their charismatic personalities work well to persuade employees to help them put their plans into action and achieve success. These individuals work well under adverse conditions, and they are often the best choice for plant manager positions when organizations are experiencing difficult times.

Disadvantages

Transformational plant managers are not very detail-oriented because they tend to focus on the big picture. Their lack of attention to detail can negatively affect the long-term vision they have in mind...even to the point where it does not work.

Additionally, these plant managers are not always honest about their organization. Their charismatic personalities and passion for their vision often cause them to ignore reality. If employees detect this dishonesty, they can lose faith and trust in the plant manager's objectives.

Not surprisingly, plant managers' organizational skills include more than leadership. They also involve their ability to organization processes and product flow. An example is inventory control. Plant managers need to have inventory processes in place that assure:

- Finished product stock is maintained at sufficient levels. Too much inventory results in unnecessary cost and too little inventory results in unfulfilled customer orders. Inventory is expensive, but so are lost customer sales...so there needs to be a balance.
- Raw materials are maintained at sufficient levels. Without raw materials, finished products cannot be manufactured and sales are lost.
- Theft, damage, and other losses are minimized. These types of problems negatively affect the bottom line...and the job of the plant manager.

Product warehousing also requires processes that need to be organized by plant managers. Warehouses are areas where products are stored after they are packaged and before they are sold to customers. They are a necessary part of most manufacturing businesses because those businesses need inventory to fill customer orders.

Warehouses are typically very structured. They have designated areas for every product so employees have an idea of where they need to go when they fill customer orders. For example, a furniture manufacturing warehouse has bedroom furniture in one area and office furniture in another area. Additionally, most warehouses store the oldest products in the front to assure proper rotation. Plant managers need processes in place to assure that this rotation happens.

Products in inventory are often designated by stock-keeping units (also known as SKU). SKUs contain product numbers, product types, and product descriptions. This allows employees to search by barcode labels using scanning guns, which is much easier and faster than visually searching for products. Without organization, this process will not be efficient...and responsibility for that efficiency falls on the shoulders of plant managers.

Another example of organizational skills needed by plant managers involves product packaging. People who are not directly involved in the manufacturing of products probably do not think about packaging. After all, they make purchases for the product inside...not the surrounding packaging material. They usually do not notice that the packaging of a product is high quality because they expect it to be that way. However, they will notice a problem with the packaging very quickly if it does do what it is supposed to do. For example, a broken tamper resistant seal on an aspirin bottle usually results in consumers refusing to buy that product. Those consumers search for a good seal, purchase a similar product, or purchase the same product elsewhere.

Plant managers must realize that packaging rests on meeting consumer demands, and they have to organize packaging related processes based on those demands. They need to take into account the following four major factors:

- *Technological advances*

    Technology affects virtually every aspect of manufacturing in some way, shape, or form...and packaging is no exception. Durability, strength, tear resistance, tamper resistance, oxygen permeability, and moisture permeability are all examples of packaging characteristics that have been impacted by technology. These features and many others continue to improve with technological advancements, but the largest impact will likely be the way these packages are manufactured after the advancements have been implemented.

    The biggest manufacturing advancement in terms of technology is 3D printing. This process has the potential to completely transform the packaging world by printing materials on demand. At the moment, 3D printing is too costly to be used the majority of packaging manufacturers. However, like any other new technology, the price will eventually go down as the technology improves. When that happens, manufacturers will use this process in many different ways including individualizing packaging for the masses. This might sound impossible, but it is not. It will happen, and it not that far off...and plant managers need be ready to implement the required changes.

- *Regulatory intervention*

    Plant managers must understand that due to consumer demands, regulatory agencies are requiring more from packaging. For example, products from food manufacturers require detailed ingredient statements and nutritional facts panels. All ingredients need to be listed with nothing hidden from the consumer, and specific nutritional information is required.

    There are also regulations regarding the chemical make-up of packaging materials. Materials considered to be carcinogenic or dangerous in any way to people's health are being banned on a regular basis, and plant managers must have the ability to react.

    Last, but certainly not least, physical packaging standards need to be implemented. Strength testing is required to assure packaging material can hold up under normal conditions. For example, a corrugated box for a 50 lb barbecue grill might need to show that the handles do not tear under the stress of the weight when it is being carried by a person. In short, the government is involved with packaging, and manufacturers have no choice other than to conform.

- *Environmental concerns*

    No industry can escape the monitoring of environmental watchdogs. These scrutinizing groups are becoming stronger and more vocal, and they show no indication of backing down. Unfortunately, this scrutiny negatively impacts the packaging industry since a major focus is put on the recycling of packaging materials. Plant managers need to understand that manufacturers need to invest time and effort into creating recyclable materials that meet the demands of environmentalists.

- *Cost*

    Environmental concerns, technology, regulatory intervention, and consumer demands combine to make packaging costs higher than they have ever been in the past. Plant managers must understand that this cost cannot always be passed on to consumers, so other avenues need to be explored to absorb it. One such avenue involves condensing or concentrating products. Concentrated products require less packaging material, thereby lowering the unit cost. An example includes concentrated laundry soap.

    Another avenue involves lighter materials. At first glance, this might seem like it would do nothing, but plant managers need to realize that it has three distinct benefits. First, it reduces the use of the raw materials. If a package is 20 percent lighter using the same material, then 20 percent less of that material is used, and the cost is lowered. Second, lighter packaging saves storage space. More packages can be warehoused in the same amount of warehouse space. Third, lighter packaging saves transportation costs. More units can be shipped for the same amount of money, thereby lowering the overall transportation costs.

One last example that shows the need for plant manager's organizational skills involves quality assurance. Quality assurance personnel develop procedures for making sure products meet specified requirements. These procedures prevent defects and assure customers that the products they purchase adhere to pre-established criteria. They also increase consumer confidence in manufacturing. Plant managers need to have the ability to organize quality assurance departments so their products remain competitive in markets that demand uniformity.

Recruitment

Most manufacturing facilities need to recruit employees, and plant managers oversee the process. This means that plant managers need some recruitment skills in order to select the best people for the jobs available. They often interview candidates and make decisions about whether or not they are a good fit for the organization. This might seem like a relatively simple and straightforward process, but there is actually a lot of work that goes on before, during, and after the interview. This work consists of:

- *Specification*

    Every job that needs to be filled must have some type of pre-determined specifications. Plant managers need to be able to review the job in order to establish the skills, education, experience, and personality required for the best job fit. This is especially important for newly developed positions because there is no existing information available.

- *Strategy*

    This refers to the strategy used to promote job openings. Who is the job geared toward? Will the job be open to internal candidates only or can anyone apply? Will websites, social media, trade magazines, newspapers, and/or outside agencies be utilized to promote the opening? Plant managers need to ask these or similar questions to provide a method by which potential candidates can be viewed and contacted for interviews.

- *Selection*

    Plant managers must be able to reduce the candidate pool during the interview process. They need to design questions to uncover information that might not show on a resume. Leadership and interpersonal abilities are brought to light, and specific personality testing is sometimes utilized.

    Interestingly, some plant managers take the personality aspect of job fit very seriously because people's traits have been found to predict their behavior at work. Testing is utilized to determine how individuals work alone, work in teams, and work in specific environments. In other words, it shows how potential employees fit into the culture of the organization. While personality testing is not completely reliable, it does provide insight into the selection process that cannot be obtained by reading resumes or interviewing candidates.

In terms of recruiting, plant managers must have the ability to establish heterogeneous workforces that stimulate creative and innovative problem solving due to the unique strengths of each employee. However, plant managers also need to understand that while diversity is good for improving organizations as a whole, it can lead to legal and ethical concerns. People with different cultural values, customs, religious beliefs, and social norms can offend each other without even knowing it...especially if the organization is global. Bribery, for example, may be considered unethical in the United States, but it is an accepted practice in some other nations. Along the same lines, derogatory treatment of women in business might be acceptable in certain areas of the globe, but it is illegal in the United States.

One last important aspect related to recruiting skills involves bias. Plant managers must be able to steer away from any type of favoritism in order to select the best candidates for the jobs. They must avoid giving preferential hiring treatment based on personal or work relationships. This is sometimes difficult, and that is why it truly is a skill.

Motivation

Plant managers oversee many employees in manufacturing facilities. These people perform a variety of different tasks, and they need be motivated in order to perform at optimal leaves...especially if their jobs are repetitive and mundane. For this reason, motivational skills are important for plant managers.

Plant managers can motivate employees in a variety of different ways. One method involves the use of work-life balance. Work-life balance helps employees accomplish work-related goals while enjoying their lives outside of work. As their lives get busier and more hectic, workers begin to realize the importance of work-life balance. Time is limited, and different things need to take priority at different times in their lives. People know that that they need to work in order to sustain a certain lifestyle...but they also need the time to enjoy that lifestyle.

Plant managers need to understand that work-life balance benefits their workforce in many ways including:

- *Reduced stress*

    In order to understand the benefits offered here, it is best to first obtain a better understanding of the negative effects of stress in the workplace. These include:

    Fatigue

    When stress is too much, it wears on employees. They look tired and feel exhausted. When they go to bed at night, they are kept awake thinking about the issues that are bothering them. In the morning, they wake up well short of refreshed and have to deal with another stressful day.

    Anxiety

    Excessive stress causes employees to worry about issues. They fret over what might happen or what has already occurred. Worrying is often difficult to control, and sometimes it makes absolutely no sense...like when people agonize about things that might transpire. This worrying is not justified because potential issues are not for certain, and they are beyond people's control. Heavy stress, however, brings worrying to the forefront, and it is can do a lot of unnecessary damage including the hindering of job performance.

    Irritability

    One of the most common negative effects of heavy stress at work involves anger and hostility. When employees experience difficulties that they can't seem to overcome, their unpleasantness toward others is a natural side effect. This hostility can be directed at customers, suppliers, or employees...and it is rarely justified. In fact, most times this type of behavior is based solely on the fact that people are under a lot of pressure.

    Deteriorating physical health

Employees under large amounts of stress at work tend to be consumed with their jobs. They spend more and more time trying to overcome obstacles as the list of unresolved issues gets longer. In essence, they are now living to work, instead of working to live. This results in health issues such as weight loss and high blood pressure. If left unchecked, those problems can lead to much bigger concerns including malnutrition, heart disease...and possibly even death.

Employees experiencing work-life balance are able to step away from their jobs and enjoy life. They worry less, and this helps them go to sleep without thinking about work related problems. In the morning, they awake refreshed and ready to meet new challenges.

Work-life balance also makes employees less hostile and irritable because they focus on enjoyable aspects of their lives rather than the problems they experience at work. This reduces dysfunctional conflict in organizations and promotes better physical health by reducing worry and apprehension.

Plant managers need to realize that work-life balance produces happy employees, and happy employees are typically less stressed than those who are unhappy.

- *Reduced absenteeism*

Employees whose jobs are dependent on others to complete their work know how difficult it can be when the employees they depend on are absent. Job tasks become more time consuming and difficult and sometimes cannot be completed.

Individual employees are not the only ones affected by absenteeism. It impacts the entire organization by making it less efficient. Employees are hired for a reason, especially in today's lean times, and their absence breaks a link in the organizational chain that is difficult to repair. In short, absenteeism is very important to organizations because the bottom line is negatively affected when employees are not at work.

Absenteeism improves when employees find work-life balance. They enjoy their lives more and want to show up for work. They also have a stronger desire to achieve the goals and objectives of the organization.

- *Reduced turnover*

Turnover is the process of losing and replacing employees. It is a concern for many manufacturers because it adds cost to an employer's bottom line. Employees who leave an organization typically need to be replaced, and the replacements need to be trained. There is a cost to that training, and that cost becomes higher as turnover increases.

Another concern with turnover involves errors. During training, mistakes happen...and those mistakes can be very expensive. Experienced employees tend to make fewer mistakes, and this helps an organization function more efficiently.

Work-life balance reduces turnover by addressing the needs that employees have outside of work. Employers who show interest in the personal lives of their employees benefit because those employees choose to remain employed at the organization. Their experience is valuable, and the cost for replacing it negatively impacts the bottom line.

- *Increased morale*

    Employee morale is the outlook employees have about their workplace. It involves their thoughts about the work they perform and their job satisfaction. When employees' morale is lowered, their drive to achieve organizational goals decreases and their job satisfaction diminishes.

    Work-life balance programs improve employee morale by addressing their work related and non-work related needs. The end result is a win-win for the manufacturers and employees.

- *Increased productivity*

    Productivity increases when employees have work-life balance because they feel more committed to the goals of their employer. When people believe they are being treated fairly, they want to give back...and the best way to give back in a manufacturing facility is to become more productive.

Skilled plant managers clearly see that work-life balance because it is beneficial for employees and manufacturers. It produces happier and more productive employees while reducing absenteeism and turnover.

Another method of motivation involves the application of Theory Y developed by Douglas McGregor. McGregor came up with two opposite management views called Theory X (negative) and Theory Y (positive). Theory X represents the plant manager trusting only herself to do the right thing. Theory Y represents the plant manager trusting herself and her employees.

McGregor's general belief was that we should not have negative pre-conceived notions about human nature. Specifically, he thought plant managers who believed employees were lazy would make biased decisions, often counterproductive, based on that thinking (Theory X). Theory Y made positive assumptions about people, including the thinking that they would exercise self-direction and assume responsibility if committed to organizational objectives.

Four basic assumptions sum up the premise of each theory. Under Theory X, the following negative assumptions are made:

- *Employees dislike work and try to avoid it.*
- *Employees need to be coerced, controlled, or threatened for task accomplishment.*

- *Employees elude responsibility and always need direction from supervision.*
- *Employees are not ambitious and prefer job security over innovation.*

Under Theory Y, the following positive assumptions are made:

- *Employees like work and look forward to it.*
- *Employees are self-directed for task accomplishment.*
- *Employees look for responsibility and are autonomous.*
- *Employees are creative and seek out novel ways to accomplish goals and expand horizons.*

As can be seen by Theory Y, employees are motivated to perform their jobs to the best of their abilities when they are trusted. Plant managers need to have the skills necessary to motivate employees, and those who succeed realize trust is critical.

The third method of motivation that can be used by plant managers involves setting goals for employees. A theory about goal setting was developed by psychologist Edwin Locke, and it is one of the most widely known and respected theories in organizational psychology. Locke's work helped people understand motivation at work and job satisfaction, and it has been applied in a variety of different manufacturing situations. In short, Locke thought employees should set difficult and specific goals, and those goals would lead to higher work performance. This theory challenges the idea that employees should simply "do their best" since that type of thinking does not motivate people to perform optimally.

Using goal setting as a motivational tool requires discretion on the part of plant managers because it has some limitations. For example, if employee goals differ from that of the manufacturer, then the resulting conflict could cause their job performance to suffer. Additionally, employees can become so obsessed with meeting their goals that they resort to inappropriate or unethical behavior to accomplish them. Based on this, it is rather obvious that plant managers who experience success with goal setting truly are skilled.

Communication

Plant managers have to work with employees, department managers, and senior management. This requires communication skills. That being said, plant managers must have the skills necessary to overcome barriers to effective communication. Communication barriers are roadblocks to understanding the meaning of messages sent from sender to receiver. In other words, they hinder communication between people.

Barriers to communication cause a wealth of problems that decrease efficiency in manufacturing facilities. Misunderstanding prevents tasks from being accomplished; thereby hindering the achievement of organizational goals and objectives. When goals are not accomplished, manufacturers become stagnant...and some even cease to exist.

Workplace communication is influenced by a variety of different factors. Three major factors that need to be understood by plant managers include:

- *Noise*

    Many different kinds of noise create distractions in manufacturing workplaces. These distractions hinder communication by causing employees to misinterpret messages. Examples include telephones, faxes, production machinery, coworker conversations, customer visits, interviews, vendor appointments, audits, facility tours, music, and loudspeaker systems.

- *Hierarchy*

    Authority has a direct impact on communication in manufacturing facilities. Some employees high up on the corporate ladder do not make an effort to communicate with those on lower rungs. Interestingly, the opposite is also true. Some employees at lower levels do not try to communicate with those in higher positions. This makes absolutely no sense from an organizational communication standpoint, but it does happen quite frequently. These groups think of themselves as distinct, and they only communicate with coworkers on the same level.

- *Words*

    Certain words used in manufacturing workplaces are esoteric. This means they have meaning to people who possess specialized knowledge, but they are confusing to other individuals. For example, jargon results from words or expressions used in a particular trade, industry, or profession. They are very specific, and generally not understood by outsiders. An example is *trimmed to the blue* (a meat processing term that means all the fat has been removed from a ham during manufacturing).

    Along the same lines as esoteric words, acronyms are abbreviations that represent specific words or phrases. FDA (Food and Drug Administration) is an example that is understood by a fairly wide variety of people. However, the majority of terms in this category are far less familiar...especially those from the military. Examples include NFO (Naval Flight Officer), DFAC (Dining Facility), and BCD (Bad Conduct Discharge).

Plant managers need the skill to break down and classify communication barriers for better understanding. The classification is as follows:

- *Selective perception*

    This involves employees who see and hear only what they want to see and hear. They do not consider any opposing, contradictory, or differing viewpoints because they have established a position where change is not an option. This is a barrier to communication because bias results when all viewpoints are not considered.

- *Emotional status*

    People interpret and send messages differently based on the emotions they are experiencing. For example, anger causes people to hear only what they want to hear, depression causes them to shut out others, fear causes them to analyze every word spoken, and nervousness causes them to lose focus of what is being said. Emotional status is a barrier to communication because it influences manufacturing employees' actions and reactions.

- *Filtering facts*

    This occurs when employees manipulate or change information so that it is received more favorably. For example, a worker who tells the plant manager that he rarely consumes alcohol would be filtering facts if he drinks every weekend. This is a barrier to communication because information is not being received accurately.

- *Information overload*

    This happens when people have too much information to process in their minds. Employees experiencing information overload essentially ignore information (they ignore all information and simply "walk away" from the matter), select information (they reject information that they designate as unimportant in order to pay closer to information that they designate as important), or forget information (they lose track of information and cannot remember what others have told them).

    Information overload is a barrier to communication because people do not process all of the information they receive. This causes important aspects of discussions to be overlooked, ignored, or forgotten. Plant managers need the skill to overcome this barrier.

- *Language differences*

    As noted earlier, jargon and acronyms are examples of how words have different meanings to people. Language differences encompass jargon and acronyms...but they also include everyday words that are not specific to a trade, profession, or industry. For example, a young employee who says a new machine is "sick" means it is very cool, but a fifty-year-old employee views the word "sick" in a more negative light.

    In short, language is not uniform, and confusion is possible when people think everyone shares a similar perception of the same words. Based on this, one can see that language differences present a barrier to communication for plant managers.

- *Nonverbal misunderstanding*

    Nonverbal communication is discussed in the politics section of this book, but it also deserves mention here because it involves actions other than words that lead to confusion. Two subdivisions of nonverbal misunderstanding include written words and nonverbal actions. The following examines each of these in more detail:

    Written words

Written communication uses words in a variety of documents including letters, memos, reports, instructions, legal documents, and signs. The information can be handwritten, typed, or professional developed, and it can be composed using word processors, computers, email, texting, tweeting, or instant messaging. Regardless of the method used to compose and display the wording, written communication transfers information to others in writing.

Written words are not understood and interpreted the same way by everyone. They are a barrier to communication because they can create misunderstanding in the workplace...and skilled plant managers are aware of this barrier.

Nonverbal actions

This involves virtually every aspect of nonverbal communication that is not written. Body movements, gestures, expressions, positions, and appearance are all part of non-verbal actions. Voice tone, pitch, and quality also fall into this category because they are not spoken words.

People do not always see things the same way, and non-verbal actions can be interpreted differently based on individual perception. Plant managers need to realize that nonverbal actions present barriers to communication because they can create misunderstanding in the workplace.

- *Gender differences*

Men and women have different perceptions of situations, and this can prevent them from effectively working together. Women tend to focus on indirect ways to resolve problems, and they rely on feelings for making decisions. Men often approach problem solving in direct ways, and they rely on facts for decision making. There is no "right" or "wrong" here, but plant managers need to be aware that gender differences can create problems in the workplace.

- *Cultural differences*

Most people who have worked with cultures other than their own understand that the differences can create workplace challenges. These challenges are resolving themselves as organizations become global melting pots, but issues currently exist that negatively influence communication between employees. A good plant manager understands culture and takes actins to prevent problems.

- *Withholding information*

Some people intentionally remaining silent in order to withhold information that other employees might find useful. This can cause a variety of workplace problems, and it is often done for job security or power reasons. Plant managers need to be able to extract withheld information so it can be put to use.

- Deceitful misrepresentation

    This occurs when people purposely do not tell the truth. They manipulate facts, figures, or other information to benefit personally, and their actions cause problems in the workplace. Plant managers must be aware of employee deceit and work to discourage it.

The skill to communicate is important for most jobs, but it is critical for plant managers due to the wide variety of people that they interact with on a daily basis.

Strategic

In order for manufacturers to move forward, they need strategy...and plant managers are involved heavily in developing and implementing that strategy. In fact, plant managers are often the most important people in terms of strategy.

Strategy starts with goals because they are essentially stepping stones that work to achieve vision. These goals can be short-term or long-term, but goals in manufacturing organizations typically fall into the long-term category. They motivate employees to perform and indicate progress toward a bigger idea….that idea being the vision of the manufacturer.

Plant managers need to understand why goals are established, how they are implemented, why they are significant, and what they are used for. The following discusses each of these in more detail:

- *Reasons*

    Why do manufacturers need to set goals? Plant managers need to understand that they need to set goals because those goals help employees focus on specific tasks while working toward the greater good of their companies. This might sound rather cliché, but it is true. Employees need direction, and goals provide that direction. Employees also need motivation, and goals provide motivation through benchmarking and accomplishments. These accomplishments might be small, but they are significant because they break down organizational vision into smaller chunks that are easier to achieve than taking on the entire vision all at once.

- *Process*

    What process is needed to establish goals? Plant managers need to understand that Goals focus on organizational priorities that lead to a larger accomplishment known as vision. One of the most widely known and acceptable processes used for establishing goals is known by the acronym SMART (specific, measurable, attainable, relevant, time-bound). There are a number of variations of SMART, but the basic premise is that goals should be:

Specific

Goals need to be clear when they are established. Without clarity, it is difficult to pinpoint what it is that the organization is trying to accomplish. Specific, rather than general, goals help employees align their efforts and move into action. For example, a goal of "10 percent sales growth within one year" is better than a much broader goal of "grow sales."

Measurable

Goals also need to be quantified in order to determine their rate of success. For example, the goal of 10 percent sales growth within one year is easily measurable by comparing current year sales to previous year sales for the same time period. Measurement is important so people know what they have accomplished.

Attainable

This might be the most important aspect of SMART because goals that are not attainable are not worth setting. Unattainable goals demoralize employees and decrease their efforts resulting in overall lower productivity. However, plant managers need to refrain from setting goals that are too easily accomplished. If this happens, employees are not challenged and will not put forth their best effort.

Relevant

Goals need to have relevance for the employees trying to achieve them, and straying from that relevance often leads to problems that are difficult to resolve. For example, the goal of a sales force should not be to reduce manufacturing costs by five percent. Salespeople have no control over production related activities, and if they try to get involved they will upset production management personnel and not do what they are paid to do....which is sell products.

Time Bound

This refers to the establishment of deadlines. Goals without deadlines have no sense of urgency, and employees tend to postpone achieving them. They choose to work on other tasks that require their attention, which results in some goals never getting accomplished. Deadlines are important...and that is why so many plant managers implement them.

- *Documentation*

Why are goals documented? When goals are established, they need to be put in writing to provide direction, spell out details, and prevent "he said, she said" situations from occurring. Documentation is so important that many goals fail simply because they were only established verbally.

Why are goals important for organizations? Plant managers must understand that they are important because they are:

- *Indicators*

    Plant managers typically need to look for ways to grow their organizations in order to be successful. Goals are indicators of success because they can be looked back on to see what has been achieved. If goals are completely achieved, then plant managers are successful because they accomplished what they set out to do.

- *Synergistic*

    Teamwork is a significant aspect of workplaces today because employees work together to solve problems. They feed off each other's progress as they move towards achieving goals, and each individual has something unique that they contribute. In short, multiple minds produce synergy cannot be achieved by one person thinking alone…and this is beneficial to manufacturers.

- *Informational*

    Goals provide information for decision making in manufacturing. Plant managers can look back at what they have accomplished and make changes or improvements to programs, policies, processes, and/or procedures. The best part about the information provided by goals is the fact that it indicates trends rather than snapshots of progress. Plant managers need trends to see how employees have progressed, and snapshots only provide a picture of the current situation. It is unfair to judge employees without having a true idea of what they have accomplished, and goals make this possible.

It is not surprising that goals require planning. That planning starts at the top of the hierarchy, and the top of the hierarchy in manufacturing is the plant manager. Strategical planning applies to the entire organization. It establishes mission, defines short-term and long-term goals, and provides a framework for employees to expand upon. Plant managers need to design and implement plans so the objectives can be supported by lower level employees. In short, Plans are a roadmap for taking a manufacturer from where it is to where it wants to be in the future.

Plant managers must be aware that planning is never a simple process because it involves risk. Since manufacturers experience a wide variety of risks, decisions need to be made based on the potential rewards or consequences. Plant managers do this by implementing programs known as risk management. These programs are designed to reduce uncertainty in organizations when the effects of something that might happen are unknown. This is important because negative effects can compromise the goals and objectives of organizations…and they can even lead to manufacturers shutting down.

Uncertain times have led many manufacturers to stop forecasting or predicting their future. Economic downfalls, environmental concerns, and political changes have all impacted the way business is conducted, and this has led to plant managers being more discrete about their short-term and long-term plans. Uncertainties have also resulted in plant managers choosing to focus more on risk management than they have ever done in the past. They try to identify the most significant risks in their organizations and act accordingly with programs designed to reduce or eliminate them.

Essentially, any actions that reduce or eliminate risk fall under the umbrella of risk management. These actions help organizations secure their future by warding off potential problems before they occur. Risk management allows plant managers to make business decisions with confidence, and it also provides options when potential problems become reality. Plant managers who make decisions without evaluating risk are gambling…and that gambling can lead to the demise of their organizations.

Risk management programs also play a big role in protecting manufacturers from potential catastrophes. These programs are put in place for decision making that identifies potential danger and works toward preventing or eliminating it. In short, they help organizations achieve goals and objectives while controlling the risks involved.

Plant managers need to implement six basic steps when establishing risk management programs. These steps are as follows.

- *Assemble*

    This step involves assembling the risk management team. Care needs to be taken when selecting people because there should be a mixture of job responsibilities and personalities that allow the team to identify and analyze risk from multiple perspectives without bias. Work experience is important because veteran employees typically have knowledge that is worth its weight in gold…and new employees often make suggestions that were previously never considered. The goal of the selection process is to make sure the team is heterogeneous so members do not all think the same. Plant managers must understand that diversity is important for assessing risk in any situation.

- *Identify*

    This is where risks are realized. Each team member identifies and documents the risks that they see in their organization. Their perception is valuable because everyone perceives things differently.

    This procedure should not take place in meetings because (1) some team members are more dominant than others and (2) there is potential for groupthink. Each member needs to think independently and document the risks they determine to be important. This asynchronous process gives all members flexibility so they can fit their thinking into their routine work schedules.

- *Analyze*

    Now the team gets together to categorize the risks that have been submitted by individual members. Some risks overlap and can be combined in the same category, others need their own separate category, and still others are eliminated. These categories define the type of risk and its potential impact on organizational goals and objectives. They also create a solid structure that helps facilitate the next step of the process (evaluate).

- *Evaluate*

    After risks have been categorized, it is time to rank them in order of importance. Typically this is done by evaluating each risk for its potential to occur and consequences that can result. Some risks are important enough to be quickly addressed in the next step while others can be moved to the backburner.

    This step is sometimes considered the most difficult because inaccurate evaluations can lead to unanticipated problems...essentially defeating the purpose of the risk management team. However, plant manager must understand that there is a need for an order of importance, and evaluation fulfills that need.

- *Address*

    Once risks have been categorized and ranked, it is time to address those that have been determined to be the most important. This is commonly referred to as response planning, and it is where the treatment begins. This treatment involves reducing the risks to acceptable levels using strategic planning and contingency planning. The goal is to minimize the probability of negative risks while determining ways to address the problems that result when risks become reality.

- *Monitor*

    At this point, the risk management team has identified, analyzed, evaluated, and addressed important risks in their organization. However, the program still needs to be monitored to assure that it is working properly.

    In this step, plant managers need to ask questions. Is the program working as intended? Are the established controls still effective? Will the established controls be effective in the future? What are the weak points? What needs to be changed? If the program has been successful, then it can be left as is without change. However, if the program has failed or the future points towards its failure, then changes need to be made.

Plant managers also need to take into account the two types of risk management in order to move forward with risk management programs. These types are quantitative and qualitative and are broken down as follows:

- *Quantitative*

Quantitative risk management determines the cost of catastrophic situations by establishing the probability of occurrence and the potential consequences resulting from that occurrence. It classifies and evaluates the impact of problems on organizations and their employees. In short, it determines the cost of lost productivity, replacement of assets, and damaged reputation using statistical analysis. For example, the meat processing risk management team might use a continuous variable commonly known as return on investment (ROI) to determine the standard deviation (variance) of a financial risk. First, they identify the threats that produce the biggest estimated losses, and then they determine appropriate measures to reduce those losses.

An advantage of quantitative risk management is the results are objective. Personal bias is not a factor because statistical analysis is used to determine risk. However, a disadvantage of quantitative risk management is the complexity of the process. Calculation of results can be difficult and cumbersome. Plant managers need to consider advantages and disadvantages before embarking on quantitative risk management analysis.

- *Qualitative*

    Qualitative risk management does not utilize statistical analysis and is therefore used by many small organizations. It uses relative values to determine potential loss if a problem occurs. In short, it awards scores for the probability of problematic situations and the need for action to minimize the risk involved. For example, the meat processing company is located in rural Kansas. The risk management team might evaluate the probability of a hurricane as insignificant and the need to take action to reduce the risk as very minor. Along the same lines, they might evaluate the probability of employees missing work as very likely and the need to take action to reduce risk as major.

    Advantages of qualitative risk management include ease of calculation and implementation. The method is relatively simple to understand and implement in most organizations. However, a major disadvantage is personal bias. Lack of statistical analyses allows employees the ability to manipulate results based on their perceptions of situations. Plant managers need to consider advantages and disadvantages before embarking on a qualitative risk management analysis.

Quantitative and qualitative types of risk management differ in some ways, but both types have a goal of identifying risks and reducing or eliminating them.

Training

Workforces in manufacturing plants need to be educated, and plant managers need to understand that that education comes from training. Training is a process where employees acquire knowledge and skills that can be used for enhancing their job performance. They get better at their jobs, thereby becoming more efficient and effective. Additionally, training leads to employees requiring less direct supervision. They are able to do their work with minimal guidance do to the autonomy that training instills. This means supervisors can focus on other aspects of their jobs without the threat of employee mistakes being made due to misunderstanding or lack of knowledge.

One benefit of training that largely goes unnoticed involves psychology. Plant managers need to understand that training improves attitudes and increases morale because employees feel empowered due to the attention paid to them. They realize that they are more than just a "face in the crowd," and their jobs have an impact on the well-being of the organization. Attention also works well for increasing employee commitment. They feel an active part of the organization, and this makes them more committed toward its goals and objectives.

Plant managers need to be aware that there are a variety of advantages for manufacturers that conduct employee training. Some of these are rather obvious, while others less noticeable. However, regardless of the visibility, these advantages are important…and they are the reasons why organizations choose to put money, time, and effort into training.

The following are positives that result from employee training:

- *Increased skills*

    In many instances, this is the most obvious advantage because the reason for training is usually to increase employee skills. Plant managers want their workers to do their jobs more efficiently and effectivity, and this requires up-to-date knowledge and understanding of the tasks they perform. That knowledge and understanding are best obtained using some form of employee training.

    The most important part about increased employee skills is the fact that they benefit employees and plant managers. Workers benefit by becoming more knowledgeable and valuable in their chosen profession, and plant managers benefit by having more competent employees to help meet workplace goals and objectives.

- *Increased motivation*

    Motivation is important in any manufacturing workplace because it drives employees to perform at optimum levels. Without motivation, workers lack the desire to complete job-related tasks…and this prevents organizations reaching their potential.

    Training allows employees to learn new concepts and better understand the requirements of their jobs. This enables them to work with limited supervision, and the resulting autonomy increases their motivation.

- *Increased innovation*

    Training is designed to help people learn, and this learning builds their confidence. Confident people like to experiment and try new things, and this leads to the development of innovative ideas and concepts.

Innovation is important for employees because it keeps them interested and involved. Innovation is important to plant managers because it keeps their organizations on the cutting-edge and prevents stagnation.

- *Increased job satisfaction*

    Job satisfaction has been defined in many different ways by a variety of sources. For simplicity purposes, this book views it as employees' like or dislike of their jobs. Training leads to workers liking their jobs because it provides information that helps them complete assigned tasks. This allows them to experience success…and that success increases their job satisfaction.

- *Increased collaboration*

    Many employees like to share newly acquired knowledge about their jobs. After all, this knowledge has the greatest value in the workplace because other people are working toward achieving the same goals.

    Training provides manufacturing employees with new knowledge, and that knowledge is shared through collaboration with coworkers. This collaboration encourages workers to think differently due to the diversity of the people involved, and the resulting ideas are beneficial for the growth and prosperity of the organization.

- *Decreased long-term costs*

    There is a cost associated with any type of training. Manufacturers spend time and money educating employees and, in the short term, this can seem expensive. However, that expense is easily recouped in the future because employees do not waste time trying to figure out how to perform job-related tasks for which they were trained. Workers also save the organization money by performing the tasks correctly the first time around.

    In reality, training saves time and money by decreasing workplace costs. Plant managers who understand the long term benefits of training realize that it is a good investment for the future of their organizations.

- *Decreased absenteeism and turnover*

    Training can be a double-edged sword in terms of turnover. It provides knowledge, and that knowledge can be used to find a better job at another organization. However, this is typically not the case because training inspires loyalty in employees….and that loyalty keeps them working for their current employer.

    Along the same lines, training also reduces absenteeism. The new knowledge employees acquire inspires them to show up for work and do their jobs. Knowledge truly is power…and workers cannot use that power if they are not at work.

Decision making

Decision making is very important in organizations. In fact, it is so important that wrong decisions made by plant managers can cause manufacturers to go out of business if they do not have the necessary resources to survive the consequences. However, everyone knows that wrong decisions can have detrimental effects on workplaces. The real challenge lies in knowing in advance which decisions will have the most impact on the fate of organizations...and that is why it is an essential skill for plant managers.

There are many variables that influence plant manager's decisions. It is virtually impossible to list all of these because everyone has unique reasons for making choices. However, there are some common factors that play a major role, and these factors are as follows:

- *Ethics*

    Some decisions are made based on ethical concerns. For example, a plant manager might decide not to purchase goods from a supplier that exploits immigrant workers in their factories. Decisions such as the one in this example are made to adhere to certain principles.

- *Resources*

    Resources include money, people, and time...and they can all be in short supply and high demand. For example, a plant manager might decide not to build a new plant because he is uncertain of the return of investment. Decisions such as the one in this example this are made to conserve resources that might are needed elsewhere.

- *Quality*

    Some organizations value quality above just about anything else. They work hard to maintain an image of offering the best products or services available, and their decisions reflect this effort. For example, a plant manager at a bakery might decide that she is going to use real butter in her scones and croissants regardless of the price. Her customers view real butter as high quality, and they frown on substitutes like margarine. Decisions such as the one in this example are made to maintain the integrity of organizations.

- *Experience*

    This involves making decisions based on similar past experiences. For example, assume there is a leak in the ceiling of a manufacturing facility. Experience tells the plant manager to check the overhead steam pipes first because they have broken in the past. Decisions such as the one in this example are made based on understanding of the situation.

- *Bias*

Unfortunately, bias is a major contributor to decision making. Assume the plant manager does not personally like a particular supervisor. Based on this dislike, the plant manager often decides against suggestions made by this supervisor regardless of the fact that some of those suggestions are good for a manufacturing facility. Decisions such as the one in this example are made to satisfy the ego of individuals.

Bias is often the most damaging factor because it does not allow plant managers to forego their personal beliefs and make the best decisions for the organization. In fact, bias is often a major reason why facilities shut down. Plant managers of failed manufacturers only hear and see what they want to hear and see, and this leads to their inability to make unbiased decisions.

- *Age*

Believe it or not, age plays a role in decision making. Older plant managers tend to make more conservative decisions than younger plant managers. This is partially due to the experience of older people, but it also stems from the fact that they do not want to fail and be forced to start all over again. Decisions like these are made based on the risk willing to be taken by the plant manager.

- *Environment*

Some decisions are made based on environmental concerns. For example, a manufacturer might own land in a pristine area of Alaska. They have every right to build a new plant on this land, but the plant manager decides not to do so because it would upset people and politicians who strongly believe the land should be left undisturbed. Decisions such as the one in this example are made to establish or preserve the image of organizations.

- *Policies*

Policies and procedures often dictate decisions. For example, a plant manager might be asked about an employee's religious beliefs. By law and company policy, the plant manager cannot divulge this information to another party. Decisions such as the one in this example are made to protect organizations from lawsuits.

- *Hierarchy*

Authority at higher levels in organizations often impacts lower level employee decision making. For example, a plant manager might decide to accept a promotion that involves relocation to another division of a consulting company because he knows this is what upper management wants him to do. He is told the decision is his to make...but he understands that he might never again be considered for a promotion if he declines the offer. Decisions such as the one in this example are made to protect the careers of plant managers.

- *Government*

Government agencies have a big impact on decision making. For example, the plant manager might decide to put sewer drains in her parking lot because the city requires proper drainage of the lot. She does not want to add the drains because are costly, but they are mandated by local code requirements. Decisions such as the one in this example are made to prevent organizations from facing the consequences of violating government rules or regulations.

- *Economy*

    The economy tends to affect every organization in one way or another, and it has a direct impact on decisions made by people in those organizations. For example, poor economic conditions might cause a plant manager to pull his organization's money out of stocks and invest it in bonds. He does this because bonds typically perform better than stocks when the economy is bad. Decisions such as the one in this example are made to prevent the loss of money during challenging time periods.

Plant managers constantly make decisions, but these decisions do not all carry the same weight in terms of importance. Critical decisions, typically those that affect the direction of the manufacturers, need to be made by the plant manager. Decisions of lesser importance, such as those that are governed by rules or protocol, can be delegated to lower level employees.

Determining the importance of a decision requires skill, and part of that skill involves the plant manager's ability to break decisions into the following types:

- *Routine*

    Routine decisions, also known as programmed decisions, are decisions made based on established rules or procedures. For example, the plant manager decides that the customer service department at a toy manufacturer must immediately refer all complaints involving injuries to children to the legal department. This is done because the company's attorneys are experienced handling these types of complaints, and they know what to say and what not to say to the customer.

- *Non-routine*

    Non-routine decisions, also known as non-programmed decisions, are new decisions made because there are no established rules or procedures. For example, a plant manager at a tool and die shop decides to purchase a new machine that will lower production costs by simplifying processes and procedures. Prices to customers can then be reduced, and the company will become more competitive.

- *Strategical*

    Strategical decisions are very influential because they establish goals and determine the direction of organizations. For example, plant manager decides to discontinue offering sales pricing to low volume customers. This change will save the manufacturer an estimated $250,000 annually, and it frees up money for capital expenditures.

- *Tactical*

    Tactical decisions are made after the direction of the organization has been determined. For example, a decision is made by a plant manager that employees can no longer work over 39 hours per week to avoid paying overtime. As a result of this decision, departmental supervisors require employees to report their hours on a daily basis so they can be monitored more closely.

- *Operational*

    Operational decisions are decisions made on a daily basis. They are subordinate to strategical and tactical decision and are typically made with limited impact and risk. For example, the plant manager at a soda manufacturing plant decides she needs to produce 200,000 bottles of root beer, 100,000 bottles of cola, and 50,000 bottles of grape this week. She knows she might not sell that much soda over the next seven days, but the rest can be put into inventory for future orders.

In short, skilled plant managers need to understand the risks involved with decision making and be objective. Since it is virtually impossible to pinpoint the importance of every decision, they need to utilize other people's input in order to make the best decisions possible.

Emotional intelligence

Plant managers need to listen to, understand, and empathize with their employees. This can be very challenging, but mastering these skills often separates good plant managers from those who are not so good.

Emotional intelligence is a plant manager's ability to manage his own feelings and understand the feelings of others. Plant managers with high emotional intelligence know what their emotions are capable of doing, and they harness their feelings to prevent negative reactions from others.

Emotional intelligence is a term that was developed by psychologists Peter Salovey and John Mayer...and later popularized by popularized by psychologist Daniel Goleman. Essentially, Goleman designated five major components of emotional intelligence. These components are:

- *Self-awareness*

    This refers recognizing one's own feelings. Plant managers who are self-aware are able to identify and monitor their own emotions for control. They are confident and have a good sense of humor. They are also aware of how they are perceived by others.

- *Self-regulation*

This refers to controlling reactions or impulses. Plant managers who react quickly often end up saying things that they would not have said if they thought about the situation. Self-regulation makes people conscientious about what they are saying, and it prevents them from responding in ways that elevate the negativity of conversations.

- *Motivation*

    This refers to self-motivation for self-improvement. It goes above money and status (external rewards) by focusing on things such as satisfaction and happiness (internal rewards). It also includes a strong drive to accomplish goals and objectives regardless of the circumstances. Optimism is critical for plant managers here...even when they are faced with potential failure.

- *Empathy*

    This refers to plant managers understanding other people's situations and taking a genuine interest in those situations. It often involves "walking a mile in another person's shoes" to fully comprehend their behavior and reactions. This is the most skillful component because it sometimes requires the anticipation of other's needs so the appropriate response can be made.

- *Social skills*

    This involves plant managers picking up on social cues to build relationships and work toward common goals. It requires active listening and appropriate responding to persuade others and gain their trust. It also involves team-building and collaboration as a method of working with others.

Plant managers need to realize that emotional intelligence is a great tool for preventing conflict. Not all conflict is bad because many good things come when people disagree (known as functional conflict). Without functional conflict, groupthink can result where everyone agrees because they believe it is the general consensus of the group. Groupthink prevents potential solutions from surfacing and, consequently, problems are not resolved with the best solutions. However, conflict is bad when it becomes dysfunctional. Dysfunctional conflict results in a focus on position instead of principle, and it leads to people being attacked rather than problems. Dysfunctional conflict often results in a complete breakdown of communication, and nothing constructive gets accomplished.

Emotional intelligence improves plant managers' ability to communicate constructively and collaboratively. It also helps them remain calm in challenging situations, and it prevents dysfunctional conflict from occurring. In short, emotional intelligent is needed for plant managers to perform at peak levels.

A discussion on the skill of emotional intelligence would not be complete without mentioning listening. Listening plays a big role in communication for plant managers. In fact, it might be the most important aspect of their communication because lack of it tends to create a wealth of misunderstanding.

Listening is a process that involves plant manager's focusing on what others are saying. On the surface, this might seem like an easy task…but that is typically not the case due to the barriers that are present. These barriers include noise, visual distractions, emotions, fatigue, anger, accents, language, jargon, and acronyms. All of these barriers prevent understanding and lead to misunderstanding because the message that is being sent is not comprehended.

The previous paragraph makes it seem like listening is a lost cause because it has so many barriers. Fortunately, this is not true. With a little concentration, plant managers can hear and comprehend what is being said by others. This is good because effective listening has many benefits including:

- *Understanding*

    There is no doubt that effective listening creates better understanding of the discussion that is transpiring. Without understanding, most conversations are severely hindered. Think about holding a conversation with a friend inside a crowded bar that has loud music playing. The loud music and crowd noise creates a barrier to effective listening, and the resulting lack of understanding hinders the conversation.

- *Efficiency*

    When people listen to each other, everything becomes more efficient. They understand what is being said, resulting in less confusion and fewer mistakes. In this sense, it is much easier to accomplish goals and tasks that are a part of everyday life.

- *Insight*

    When plant managers hear what is actually being said, they gather information that can be used to define position and make decisions. This information influences behavior and brings about change that helps individuals reach the mindset where they feel the most comfortable. Plant managers who do not effectively listen fail to acquire information, and they are often left uncertain of the direction they need to take on important aspects of the conversation.

- *Bonding*

    This is likely the least known benefit of effective listening, but often times it is the most important of those listed in this book. This is because trust builds when one person believes another is listening to them…and trust leads to bonding.

    Conversations also become more enjoyable when effective listening is employed because there is less repeating of what has already been said. In this regard, effective listing helps people bond because speakers feel like their words are important and not easily forgotten. They do not get annoyed from being asked to repeat the words that they have just spoken, and this prevents the potential conflict that can occur when people become upset with others for apparent lack of interest or concern.

Skilled plant managers understand that active listening means fully concentrating on the speaker while blocking out all distraction. This is a learned skill that takes work, but it can be achieved with some time and effort.

LADDER is an acronym that helps plant managers actively listen. It has been around for many years and it is often used by consultants to help people improve their listening skills. LADDER stands for the following:

- *L - Look at the person talking to you*

    Plant managers who look away from the speaker appear uninterested or bored. When this happens, speakers tend to shut down because they feel that they are not getting the proper attention paid to them. Some people even become upset because they feel insulted.

- *A - Ask questions*

    Follow-up questions need to be asked by plant managers in order to fully comprehend what speakers are saying. These questions should be open-ended so explanation and expansion on the subject matter is possible. For example, rather than asking an employee if she likes her job, it is better to ask her to explain what she likes and dislikes about her job. A simple yes or no does not always give enough information…just ask anyone who has been through a legal deposition.

- *D – Don't change the subject*

    Changing the subject is a very common mistake that plant managers make when they are supposed to be listening. For example, an employee is talking about the beautiful rivers she saw during a recent trip to Alaska, and the plant manager changes the subject to the beautiful everglades he saw during a trip to Florida. The employee feels as if the spotlight has shifted from her trip to his vacation…and this is frustrating.

- *D – Don't interrupt*

    Some plant managers have a tendency to interrupt others when they are speaking. Instead of listening, these individuals are thinking about what they are going to say next…and this interferes with their comprehension of what the speaker is saying. Interruption is sometimes necessary for clarification purposes, but it should be avoided as a general rule.

- *E - Emotions…control emotions*

Not surprisingly, plant managers need to control their emotions when listening to others. Outbursts should be avoided because they prevent effective listening and lead other problems such as disagreement or conflict.

- *R - Respond to the person speaking*

    Plant managers who engage themselves will listen more effectively because they are involved in the conversation. Fortunately, engagement can be accomplished without asking questions or interrupting. For example, plant managers can smile, nod their heads, raise their eyebrows, or lean forward showing interest. Additionally, simple phrases such as "I understand" or "that makes sense" can also be used as response techniques.

When listening on the telephone, the "L" may stand for limit doing other things such as typing, writing, using a calculator, trying to hold another conversation, or attempting to answer another call. Many plant managers like to perform multiple tasks, but often times a telephone conversation deserves their complete attention.

Plant managers must often take on a role of a psychologist as they listen to employees and comfort them or help them find their way. In fact, some plant managers work with industrial/organizational psychologists employed by the company to resolve internal employee issues.

I/O psychologists are involved in the design, execution, and interpretation of psychological research in organizations. They apply their findings to problems involving people or processes within those organizations. Not surprisingly, some of their skills are necessary for plant managers because they are related to understanding human behavior in terms of performance, personality, motivation, and ability.

These skills include the following:

- *Thinking*

    Logical and critical thinking are important for all plant managers. They need to identify workplace problems and formulate approaches those problems. Once those problems are resolved, the experience can be applied to other workplace situations.

- *Speaking*

    Speaking skills are important plant managers because they talk with people on an everyday basis. They need to convey information verbally in order to complete tasks and achieve goals. Their words, voice tone, and paralanguage affect the understanding of the information they are conveying. Plant managers who do not speak effectively leave employees confused. This prevents them from accomplishing their goals and leads to other problems in manufacturing facilities.

- *Reading*

Plant managers must be able to understand what they are a reading. They need to review employee dispute documentation, hiring procedures, company policies, and legal documents...and then use that information to propose changes for the better. Without the ability to absorb what they are reading, plant managers are not capable of performing their jobs at the highest level.

- *Writing*

The written word is important for plant managers because interpretation of the meaning can be confusing. Consider, for example, the following sentence:

Jim never said Judy stole your book.

Now notice how the meaning changes each time the sentence is read, but a different word is emphasized (the emphasized word is capitalized):

- ➢ JIM never said Judy stole your book (meaning Jim did not say Judy stole your book, but another person may have said she stole it).
- ➢ Jim NEVER said Judy stole your book (meaning Jim did not say Judy stole your book at all).
- ➢ Jim never SAID Judy stole your book (meaning Jim did not say Judy stole your book, but he implied it).
- ➢ Jim never said JUDY stole your book (meaning Jim did not say Judy stole your book, but he did say someone else stole it).
- ➢ Jim never said Judy STOLE your book (meaning Jim did not say Judy stole your book, but she borrowed it).
- ➢ Jim never said Judy stole YOUR book (meaning Jim did not say Judy stole your book, but she stole another person's book).
- ➢ Jim never said Judy stole your BOOK (meaning Jim did not say Judy stole your book, but she stole something of yours other than your book).

The above sentence shows how simply reading written words does not always convey the intended message. People who misinterpret word emphasis of the sender may change the context and distort the meaning of what they are reading. The point of this exercise is to show that plant managers need to be able to write effectively or they risk losing the intent of their messages.

Problem solving

Problem solving is an extension of decision making, but it warrants a discussion of its own because it is a core component of a plant manager's job. Manufacturing facilities experience a wealth of problems, and that is why supervisors are needed in virtually every department. Those supervisors, however, are not all capable of resolving issues within their own jurisdiction, so they seek out the assistance of a higher up individual known as the plant manager.

Problem solving skills are an absolute must for plant managers because, without them, they cannot do their jobs effectively. They need to assess a wide variety of different problems and act accordingly...which is typically much easier said than done. In order to better understand the overall skill of problem solving, it is best to break it down into the following sub-skills:

- *Investigation skills*

    Managers in every organization need investigation skills in order to resolve problems. However, plant managers must be able to quickly ascertain problems and resolve them on a moment's notice. In manufacturing facilities, factors such as production deadlines, sales promotion demands, machinery downtime, and product scheduling issues all make time management a critical aspect of the investigating process. Plant managers who lack the ability to properly manage their time will find the investigation process much more difficult; thereby making it challenging to solve problems

- *Mechanical skills*

    Mechanical skills are important for problem solving because manufacturing operations use production machinery to assemble products. These machines break down over time, and the pace is often fast and furious. However, broken machines are not a major issue if they can be fixed, so plant managers must understand what needs to be done in order to get those machines running properly in a reasonable amount of time. This saves manufacturers money, and it allows them to get their products to the customers who need them.

- *Project management skills*

    Project management is exactly what it says...it is the management of projects. In order to be properly managed, every project needs a plan of action... and plant managers are in charge of developing that plan.

    An example of a project where a plant manager's skills are needed is a bakery. The objective of the bakery is to establish a new production line for pretzels. More specifically, this line must be able to manufacture 600 pretzels per hour or 4800 pretzels in an eight-hour shift. This objective needs to be kept in mind by the plant manager throughout the project to assure it is accomplished. For example, if an engineer determines that the line is only capable of producing 3200 pretzels in an eight-hour shift, then the plant is obligated to stop the project from moving forward until the necessary changes are made to meet productivity standards. The following are other factors that the plant manager must keep in mind:

    Materials

    Materials for the pretzel line project need to be managed, and this involves asking questions. What materials will be needed? Has everything been ordered? When will the materials arrive? Where will the materials be stored? All of these questions need to be answered for the project to flow smoothly. Plant managers might not do the actual ordering or inventorying of the materials, but they need to oversee the overall process.

People

People involved in the project need to be identified...regardless of whether they are company employees or contracted workers. Again, this involves asking questions. Who will be needed to complete the pretzel line project? When and where will they be needed? People involved in design, engineering, employee safety, food safety, quality assurance, and testing will all need to be part of the pretzel line, and their involvement needs to be managed. Plant managers need to tap the expertise of all of these individuals to keep the project moving forward. They do not need to do the actual work because the people are qualified to do their jobs, but those people need to be told when and where their services are needed.

Timeframe

Some projects tend to go on forever, and this is usually is due poor management. Plant managers need to establish time frames for completion so people are aware of what they need to do and where they need to be in terms of accomplishing tasks. The time allotted for the pretzel line is 120 day from the start of the project. The required raw materials (ingredients, packaging, boxes, etc.) must be in the bakery 90 days after the project has started, and test product must be run within 100 days. Based on these requirements, product will be ready to hit the store shelves within the 120-day timeframe.

Cost

Cost is a factor for most activities in organizations, and it needs to be a factor for the pretzel line. It has been determined that the total cost for the pretzel line must not exceed $200,000. This includes design, production equipment, installation, and testing. If the cost exceeds $200,000, then the plant manager is obligated to stop the project from moving forward until a decision to spend the extra money has been made. For example, the CEO of the bakery needs to sign off in order for the additional funding for the project to be approved.

Evaluation

This is done after the pretzel line project has been completed. Did everything go as planned? Were there major problems? If so, what needs to be changed now and for similar projects in the future? The plant manager needs to make sure this does not turn into a "blame game" where people are singled out for problems or mistakes. The goal is to evaluate the project, make improvements, and note changes for the future.

- *Innovative skills*

Product managers must understand that innovation adds value to manufacturing. This value can be internal or external, and it is often complex because it cannot always be defined by a single event. For example, product development often involves testing different prototypes in different markets to find where there is consumer demand. If a new product is scrapped because it did not work in the first market it was tested in, then there is no innovation...there is only an idea. In short, plant managers need the ability to come up with new ideas or improve concepts that already exist.

Some people think that innovation is only important for technology-based companies. While it is critical for these types of businesses, it also has significance for manufacturing. No manufacturer wants to become obsolete, and to avoid this they need to be innovative.

Some of the benefits offered by innovation include:

Increased productivity

> Innovation drives people to work harder, and that is why innovative manufacturing facilities have more productive employees. Manufacturers that are constantly looking to implement ideas and concepts need more from their employees, and those employees rise up to the occasion when they are allowed to be innovative.

Increased motivation

> The explanation for this benefit is fairly simple and straightforward. People are inspired to work for innovative manufacturers because they like being involved in projects that are new or different. Novel ideas and concepts are constantly being put into action, and this motivates employees to do their jobs to the best of their ability.

Increased creativity

> Creativity fuels innovation, but if that creativity is wasted if it is not put into action. Innovative manufacturers have people on staff who are qualified to ensure ideas are put into action. This does not guarantee success, but it assures creators that their ideas will be taken to the next level.

> In short, employees that work for innovative manufacturers are more likely to be creative because they know their ideas will be followed

through on. This gets creative juices flowing and opens doors to new ways of thinking.

Increased competitiveness

Consumers purchase products in order to make their lives easier. The internet has made them more informed than they ever were in the past and it also gives them a variety of options. Innovation gives manufacturers an advantage because it keeps them on the cutting edge and ahead of the competition.

- *Continuous improvement skills*

Continuous improvement employs the thinking that everything can be improved. In other words, there is no status quo and efforts are constantly made to raise the bar. Some of the changes resulting from this process are immediately apparent, while others are not so obvious and take time to transpire. Changes that transpire over time are often the preferred method of continuous improvement because they allow employees time to adjust to workplace modifications.

Of all the advantages, continuous improvement is the easiest to understand because it is the ultimate goal of plant manager. Designated processes and procedures continually search for problems so they can be brought to light, resolved, and prevented from reoccurring. This constant vigilance means manufacturers continue to progress and produce better products.

Sales

Sales might seem like a skill that plant managers would not need. After all, their job is to make products...not sell them. Plant managers are responsible for production, but they still need selling skills. They need to sell employees, investors, and customers.

Socially skilled plant managers know how to establish and maintain good relationships because they are able to read other's actions and modify their own behavior based on those actions. They also know how to use relationships to meet new people. Based on these abilities, socially skilled plant managers often make good salespeople who help manufacturers grow their businesses.

The following are areas where plant manager sales skills are beneficial:

Government interaction

All manufacturers are regulated by some type of government agency that implements rules and regulations. These rules and regulations are enforced and companies that violate them are subject to disciplinary action. Unfortunately, this disciplinary action can be quite severe....even to the point of temporarily or permanently shutting down a business. Based on this, it is fairly easy to understand that plant managers need skills to act as liaisons between manufacturers and government agencies. They are representatives of the organizations, and their actions can have a lasting impact. In this respect, plant managers act as salespeople to government agencies.

Audits

Skilled plant managers play the same role here as they do in government interactions, but the linkage is to an auditor rather than a government agency. Plant managers who oversee audits represent their employers…and their actions are reflective of those employers. Similar to government liaisons, plant managers with sales skills are beneficial in this capacity.

Public relations

The images of many organizations are based on public relations (also known as PR). Good PR improves images and drives sales upwards, while bad PR has the opposite effect. Astute plant managers understand the impact that public relations can have on their facilities, and they always keep this in mind. In essence, they sell their organizations to the public.

Morale

This might be the most overlooked way that sales skills help plant managers find success. Skilled plant managers gain their employees' trust…and workplace cultures with high levels of trust also have high levels of motivation. Motivated employees are inspired to do their jobs to the best of their abilities, and this leads to manufacturers becoming more successful in terms of productivity.

Political

The best and sometimes most important skill in this book is saved for last. It is absolutely essential for plant managers to have political skills based on the fact that they have to deal with so many different people at so many different levels of authority. They need to navigate through different personalities, cultures, religions, and beliefs while not offending these individuals and accomplishing the organizational goals and objectives. This is no small task…especially for plant managers who do not have a good grasp on political correctness.

Political correctness is a term that is familiar to most people. They understand its importance, but it also makes them feel uneasy because it presents the dichotomy of "damned if you do, damned if you don't." More specifically, people who choose to be politically correct risk losing the true meaning of their statements while those who choose to ignore political correctness risk offending others. This concern for political correctness has been around for a long time, but it is a major worry for plant managers because they want to avoid miscommunication and lawsuits.

Plant managers need to be aware that political correctness exists. They must understand that it affects organizational culture in positive and negative ways as follows:

Positives

- *Good model for young people* – Young employees are influenced by coworkers who are older and more experienced. If older workers show respect for the people they work with, then the younger workers will likely follow the same path. Plant managers must be proactive and encourage older employees to have a positive influence on their younger coworkers. The need to realize that those younger workers represent the future of the organization.

- *Promotes tolerance* – Mutual respect and understanding are necessary for people to work together and accept others. Plant managers need to understand the importance of tolerance for accomplishing goals and objectives.

- *Eliminates prejudice* – Bias is rarely, if ever, good in organizations. When employees judge each other negatively, the entire plant is impacted. Plant managers must understand that prejudice today could lead to stereotyping that becomes the norm in the future.

Negatives

- *Restricts the truth* - Employees are afraid to speak their minds for fear of being labeled insensitive, uncaring, archaic, ignorant, bigoted, or racist. Plant managers have to realize the truth is necessary in order to sort facts from fiction and solve problems.

- *Creates hypersensitivity* – Negative emotions can surface that lead to irrational decision making, warring factions, dysfunctional conflict, or organizational "witch hunts." Plant managers need to know that these types of problems affect the efficiency of the manufacturing plant.

- *Lawsuits* - Political correctness can lead to legal action being taken against individuals or organizations. Plant managers need to understand that lawsuits cost money....regardless of whether they are won or lost.

An entire book could be written on the reasons why political correctness exists, but it effectively boils down to employees communicating without offending each other. Employees are capable of offending each other while discussing a variety of different topics. However, discussions involving race, religion, politics, sexual orientation, and gender (also known as sensitive discussion) are the most likely evoke emotional responses and turn people against each other. Offense taken from these particular topics can lead to many problems including terminations and lawsuits. Plant managers need to understand that political correctness allows employees take part in sensitive discussions without offending each other...and the benefits will showcase themselves.

Plant managers also need to be aware that sensitive discussions evolve over time. Something that was politically correct at one time might be considered taboo today. For example, when the welfare system was developed it was positively thought as temporary assistance for people until they were able to find gainful employment. People were thought of as using the system for help, and they were not offended when others categorized them as welfare recipients. Today, some people on welfare are viewed as using the system so they do not have work. These individuals are thought of as abusing government assistance, and they are offended when they are categorized by others as welfare recipients...and it is not politically correct to label them as such.

A better example of sensitive discussion change involves race. Several decades ago, the word "negro" replaced the "n-word," and this was received well. In time, younger generations viewed "negro" less positively, and replaced the word with "colored." Once again, change was driven by a new generation and "colored" was replaced with "African-American." Today, "African-American" arouses emotional responses in some individuals because everyone grouped into this category is not from Africa. Lately, "people of color" has been a more politically correct choice of words.

When the wrong choice of words is used during a workplace discussion, it can offend people and trigger angry or emotional responses. Obviously, this is not always the case, but some employees do get offended and that offense can be prevented by using politically correct terminology.

The above examples indicate the importance of political correctness in the workplace. Plant managers need to effective monitor employee communication or they jeopardize the relationships that keep them productive. Political correctness exists in workplaces, and it will likely never go away. Plant managers need skills in this area so they can use political correctness as a tool for creating positive results rather than as a tool for destroying employee relationships.

Spoken words constitute a large portion of politically correct behavior in workplaces, but plant managers must realize that non-verbal communication is also involved. Personal hygiene (appearance, odors, etc.), attire (clothes, jewelry, piercings, tattoos, etc.), body language (rolling eyes, smirking, frowning, etc.), and paralanguage (voice tone, voice volume, etc.) also play a role. The following explores each of these types of non-verbal communication for a better understanding:

- *Personal hygiene*

    This involves appearance, smell, and general sanitary condition of employee's bodies. Messages are sent if people appear to have not showered or bathed in days. This offends some people, but they might be afraid to speak their minds due to the political incorrectness of telling someone that they "stink." Plant managers need to be aware of this and monitor themselves and their employees.

- *Attire*

The way people dress can offend others….meaning attire is a part of political correctness in organizations. For example, a conservative employee who wears a shirt with his favorite candidate might offend a coworker with liberal preferences. Without saying a word, the one employee is offended by another. This is why some plant managers prohibit political dress of any kind in the workplace.

Tattoos also fall into the attire category. An example is an employee who is offended by another with a religious symbol or phrase tattooed on her body. The offended employee is an atheist, and he does not appreciate religion in the workplace. While there is little that can be done to hide a tattoo in plain sight, plant managers need to understand that they can cause issues.

- *Body language*

Body language goes a long way in organizations. An example is an employee who rolls her eyes when another employee suggests the need for transgender bathrooms. The employee rolling her eyes is not being politically correct because she indicates her disdain for liberal policies due to her personal beliefs. Plant managers need to be aware of this and monitor themselves and their employees.

- *Paralanguage*

One employee can disagree with another, but it is not politically correct for one employee to scream at another. This person being screamed at could be offended or have their feeling hurt. Plant managers must realize that paralanguage is potentially destructive, and they need to take action to prevent or minimize it.

One last aspect of political correctness that warrants discussion involves organizational culture. Every manufacturing facility has unique experiences, philosophies, behaviors, norms, and values. They also have specific methods and patterns for interacting with suppliers, customers, employees, and the community. When combined, these attributes define an organization and make up its culture.

Plant managers must understand the power of culture…and the fact that they are one of the biggest influences on it. Conforming to the culture is important for raises, promotions, and other accolades. Those who choose to be non-conformists often end up on the outside. Some non-conformists leave the organization on their own terms because they cannot deal with the culture, while others are terminated because they cannot adjust. Either way, they experience the power of organizational culture and understand that it is something that is difficult to change.

Organizational culture provides guidelines for productivity, performance, quality, and political correctness. Manufacturing facilities have documented policies and procedures are in place to control many different aspects of work including productivity, performance, and quality.

However, plant managers need to realize that these policies and procedures often have little to do with political correctness. Instead, political correctness is mostly driven by unwritten rules. Employees conform because they believe it is the right thing to do...not because they are forced to do so. For example, documented policies state that sexual harassment is not tolerated, and any form of it is illegal and punishable by suspension or termination. However, "tattling" on employees is not prohibited by written policies and procedure. There is no formal punishment for "tattling," but it is often regarded as politically incorrect behavior. Employees who are thought of as tattlers are ignored or shunned in many instances because they violated a cultural norm.

Another example of culture involves using "we" instead of "I." It is not always politically correct to say "I finished the job." Instead, "we finished the job" is much better because it gives credit to others. This thinking is gaining popularity in organizations due to the increasing reliance on teams to solve problems. Plant managers must be aware that team members all have unique strengths that add diversity, and their differing viewpoints contribute to overall effectiveness. In areas where some members are weak, others are strong...and their combined efforts work together to solve problems. The synergy improves decision-making and helps teams reach goals within limited time frames. In many companies, selfishness is thought of as improper and sharing is the cultural norm. The old saying, "there's no I in TEAM" has a place in a growing number of manufacturers...and plant managers are a major influence on its existence.

The last example of culture and political correctness involves socializing. Some cultures frown on employee socializing while others encourage it. Plant managers need to understand that "employee socialization" is typically not going to be found in a written policy or procedure, but there are unofficial expectations. Employees who socialize above expected norms risk furthering their careers in their organizations. Along the same lines, employees who refuse to socialize might be thought of as outcasts; thereby jeopardizing their chances for advancement or rewards.

Summary

This book is a reference for essential skills of plant managers. These skills include the following:

- Delegation
- Organization
- Recruitment
- Motivation
- Communication
- Strategic
- Training
- Decision making
- Emotional intelligence
- Problem solving
- Sales
- Political

The above skills are important because they help plant managers do their jobs efficiently and effectively. They will continue to grow in importance as stockholders demand higher productivity with fewer resources in order to compete with overseas and outsourced manufacturing.

Congratulations! You now understand 12 essential skills for plant managers...and this book can always be used as a reference to look back on those skills.

Quality Assurance in Manufacturing
Explaining and Understanding

Louis Bevoc

Published by
NutriNiche System LLC

Louis Bevoc books...simple explanations of complex subjects

Introduction — 54
Customer satisfaction — 54
Organizational savings — 54
Clarification — 54
Quality assurance — 55
Quality control — 55
Implementation — 55
Part A — 55
Part B — 57
Advantages — 58
Continuous improvement — 58
Production — 58
Customer satisfaction — 59
Cost savings — 59
Organization — 59
Participation — 60
Challenges — 60
Production/quality conflicts — 60
The blame game — 60
Cutbacks — 61
Stress — 61
High expectations — 61
Production training — 62
Improving — 62
Draw correlations — 62
Change perception — 63
Allow self-evaluation — 63
Implement training — 63
Provide feedback — 65
Future — 65
Increased regulatory intervention — 65
Increased customer intervention — 66
Increased technology — 66
Increased globalization of standards — 66

    Increased importance on cost   67
    Increased emphasis on team work   67
    Increased ties to safety   67

Summary   68

Introduction

Some people think that quality assurance started in Japan during the 1950s due to poor perception of the products they produced. It is true that the Japanese embraced the quality concept, but they were not the first to implement it as part of the ongoing process.

The first organized form of quality assurance took place in the United States during the Second World War. The US government did not want malfunctioning equipment or supplies in the field during the heat of a battle, so they developed procedures to check defects after items were manufactured. This concept stopped defective products from being released for use, thereby preventing many problems for American troops.

After the war, the idea of quality assurance took root with non-military manufacturers, but it was modified to develop procedures for detecting defects before products were finished. Quality checks were still performed on finished items, but procedures were also implemented during the process for preventative measures. This was beneficial for two reasons:

Customer satisfaction

Similar to the military application, defects in products were eliminated before they reached the consumer. This resulted in a higher level of customer satisfaction, less complaints, and fewer returns.

Organizational savings

Since checks were ongoing, errors were discovered before the finished product stage. This meant that products did not have to be broken down and reassembled to eliminate defects. In short, the "first loss is the best loss" mentality was implemented so products could be stopped during assembly before additional time and effort was wasted attempting to complete the process.

Today, quality assurance personnel develop procedures for making sure products meet specified requirements. This assures customers that their purchases will adhere to pre-established standards, thereby increasing their confidence that they are dealing with a credible organization.

Virtually every organization employs some type of quality assurance, and many companies have separate departments for the work involved. Employees in these departments seek to improve processes by developing procedures that assure products adhere to specified quality standards. This allows organizations to sell consistent products and remain competitive in markets that demand uniformity.

Clarification

Quality assurance should not be confused with quality control. They have similar functions and are both part of quality management, but they are not the same. The following explains some of their differences:

Quality assurance

This process is used to make sure quality procedures are appropriate and in place for products. It assures the quality of products by establishing standards that prevent defects.

For example, a meat processing plant needs to make sure all hot dogs meet a color requirement. The quality assurance people develop a color chart that can be used as a standard. This chart is implemented in the plant as a mandatory color check on every batch of hot dogs prior to packaging.

Quality control

This process is used to verify the quality of products. It controls the quality of products using established standards that will detect defects.

Consider the hot dog example in the meat processing plant. Quality control technicians use the color chart developed by quality assurance people to check every batch of product prior to packaging. If the color does not match, the hot dogs are rejected.

Now that the difference between quality assurance and quality control is understood, it is time to move on to the next section on the implementation of quality assurance programs.

Implementation

Quality assurance programs are critical for manufacturers. They make sure procedures are in place to prevent defects, malfunctioning, and other finished product problems. Manufacturers without quality assurance programs need to implement them, and the following shows the two part process necessary to accomplish that implementation:

Part A

Below are the six steps necessary to put a quality insurance program in place. They do not complete the process, but they develop it and put it into action.

1. *Define objectives*

   Before a quality assurance program can be implemented, it needs a purpose. In other words, it needs to have defined goals and a concrete purpose. Once the objectives are defined, the organization understands the direction it needs to take, and the implementation process can begin.

   For example, a pet supply manufacturer decides to make a dog leash. They have done research and found that most leashes break after frequent use. This is a major problem for dog owners, so the pet supply company wants to make a better product.

2. *Define success*

   The objectives are in place, so now the dynamics need to be defined. Which product attributes are the most important? How can the monitoring of those attributes be incorporated into the quality assurance program?

   Durability is the most important attribute of the dog leash for the pet supply manufacturer, so durability must be incorporated in to the quality assurance program. This is done by developing procedures designed to measure durability during the manufacturing process.

3. *Define customer base*

   Who is going to use the dog leash? Is it geared for trainers or breeders? Is it meant for small dogs or large dogs?

   The pet supply manufacturer wants their new leash to be geared for large dogs kept as pets by families. They are not targeting trainers or breeders, and their main customer base is determined to be middle class suburban men and women who walk their dogs in parks.

4. *Define customer needs*

   Durability has already been defined as need, but other potential customer needs must also be investigated. Is there a color preference? Should the leash look fancy or practical? Is price a concern?

   The pet supply manufacturer determines that their customer base wants dark colors to hide the dirt. They also find that a fancy look is not important, and price is not a major concern.

5. *Define quality procedures*

   After the product and customer base have been defined, it is time to establish procedures for the quality assurance program.

   The pet supply manufacturer decides the leash will be dark blue in color, so they develop a color chart to measure the intensity of the blue. They also decide the leash needs to easily connect to a dog's collar, so they develop a procedure to manually check the connection every hour. Last, they want to use materials that are flexible and durable, so they develop a purchasing specification for the raw material.

6. *Define quality tools*

   Tools are the paperwork, software, instruments, and equipment needed to perform the designated procedures. They are provided to the employees performing quality checks on the product.

The pet supply manufacturer employees need the following tools to perform checks:

- Color chart
- Purchasing specification for raw materials
- Software to compute statistical deviations from specifications
- Tablet (computer) to record data, identify deviations from specifications, and list corrective actions

Part B

Now the program has been put into action. However, this does not complete the implementation process. The program still has to assure quality, so it is time to measure the data and react to the findings. This is done using the following four steps:

1. *Collect data*

    Data must be collected before it has any value. In this step, employees gather information from the procedural checks for subsequent analysis.

    The pet supply manufacturer collects a variety of different data. They obtain the number of leashes that did adhere to color requirements, the frequency of connection failures, and the occurrences where raw materials that did not meet specifications. After this information is gathered, it is used in the next step for analysis.

2. *Analyze data*

    This is where the collected data is analyzed. Findings are used to determine if original objectives are being achieved.

    Quality assurance at the pet supply manufacture examines statistics and percentages to look for trends of quality related issues. The results are then analyzed and decisions are made regarding the success of the program.

3. *Adjust procedures*

    If the program is deemed successful, then it will continue on in its current capacity. However, if poor quality trends are the result of failures, then changes to the program must be made.

    The pet food supplier finds that the leash connection device is failing at a rate of two percent. Quality assurance determines that two percent is too high for this product, so a minor mechanical adjustment is made, and the frequency of the manual check is increased from every hour to every half-hour. If the failure rate stays the same or increases over the next week, the connection will be redesigned by engineers in the organization.

4. *Monitor*

   If procedures have been adjusted and the quality is considered acceptable, then those procedures must be continuously monitored to assure that quality does not decrease.

   The pet food supply company finds the mechanical adjustment of the leash connection device is successful. The failure rate drops to below one-half percent, and this is acceptable. Based on this analysis, quality assurance changes the manual check frequency back to every hour, and they will watch the failure rate closely to assure there is no reoccurrence.

Now you have an understanding of a basic implementation procedure for a quality assurance program. The next section focuses on the reasons that this type of program is beneficial for organizations.

Advantages

There many advantages for organizations that have quality assurance plans in place. Some of these are more important than others, so the focus in this section will be on the most significant benefits. These are as follows:

Continuous improvement

Continuous improvement employs the thinking that everything can be improved. In other words, there is no status quo and efforts are constantly made to raise the bar. Some of the changes resulting from this process are immediately apparent, while others are not so obvious and take time to transpire. Changes that transpire over time are often the preferred method of continuous improvement because they allow employees time to adjust to workplace modifications.

Of all the advantages, continuous improvement is the easiest to understand because it is the ultimate goal of every quality assurance program. This advantage is apparent after a quality assurance program has been up and running for a while because the goal of always getting better turns into reality. Designated procedures and checks continually search for process and product problems so they can be brought to light, resolved, and prevented from reoccurring. This constant vigilance means organizations continue to progress and manufacture better products.

Production

One might question how production is an advantage of quality assurance programs. After all, quality procedures seem like they would hinder production processes rather than help them. Yes, quality assurance does hinder production, but only for the short term. In the long run, it improves production because problems associated with products are identified and prevented from reoccurring. This stops defects from getting into finished products, causing those products to be reworked or reproduced...at the expense of production.

Customer satisfaction

This is likely the biggest advantage of quality assurance programs. Products are manufactured so they can be sold to customers. If those customers are not happy with the items they purchase, then they return them and/or never buy them again.

Quality assurance verifies products are being manufactured according to specifications. Procedures are designed to identify discrepancies and bring attention to them. Changes are then made to address those discrepancies and prevent them from reoccurring. These changes lead to a happier customer base, increased sales, and fewer headaches for management.

Customer returns and dissatisfaction are huge negatives for organizations. They lower profitability, increase stress, and decrease moral. Customers might not always be right, but they are always important...and quality assurance brings that importance to the forefront.

Cost savings

Most manufacturers are looking for cost savings due to the highly competitive markets that they face today...and they find those savings with quality assurance programs. How does this work? It works by measuring how effectively the products are produced. Standards and procedures increase quality and consistency, ultimately leading to better products and higher sales.

Specifically, quality assurance programs:

- Decrease employee mistakes that create waste
- Decrease employee miscommunication that leads to errors
- Decrease reoccurrence of problems that lead to reoccurring costs
- Decrease customer complaints that require resources for response
- Increase employee awareness that prevents mishaps
- Increase employee efficiency that leads to higher productive
- Increase product consistency that results in fewer returns
- Increase customer demand that drives up sales volume

Quality assurance programs cost money for personnel, equipment, supplies, and other resources. However, those resources combine to make better products and reduce misunderstanding by standardizing processes and procedures. This translates to cost saving for manufacturers, and it makes the payback well worth the investment.

Organization

Workplace organization is one of the least obvious benefits of quality assurance. The processes and procedures to control quality also dictate the manner in which production is accomplished. In this respect, they act as behavioral guidelines with step-by-step processes that are followed in the same order every time a product is produced. This prevents the chaos that can result from unstructured environments....and it keeps manufacturers organized.

Organization is a sought after aspect of every manufacturer because it leads to effectiveness and efficiency in the workplace. It keeps employees on task and prevents unnecessary or unproductive activity from occurring. In short, productivity improves as organizations get better, and organizations get better with the implementation of quality assurance programs.

Participation

This refers to employee participation. If employees sense that quality assurance programs are making their organizations more successful, then they buy into the process and begin to make quality a priority. They gain a sense of responsibility and take ownership of their jobs. This change is gradual and might not be readily noticeable, but it does happen.

People who think that employees will not buy into effective quality assurance programs over time are wrong. Successful organizations all over the world have utilized quality programs to achieve goals and objectives, and this would not have been possible without employees working together toward continuous improvement.

As you can see, quality assurance programs produce a variety of benefits. However, these programs are not without problems, and that is why challenges are the focus of the next section.

Challenges

Most good things in organizations have some negatives associated with them, and quality assurance programs are no exception. Despite all of the positive aspects, there are some shortcomings. Quality control personnel face challenges that need to be overcome before the programs they implement can become successful.

These challenges include:

Production/quality conflicts

Conflict between production employees and quality personnel is likely the most common drawback of quality assurance programs. This is somewhat expected because both departments have job related tasks to complete, and those tasks are often opposite each other.

Quality assurance people implement programs that control the way products are manufactured, and many times this impedes the way production people want to do their jobs. Specific procedures dictate how jobs are performed, and those procedures are not always the easiest or most convenient.

The blame game

It is very easy to place blame for finished product problems on quality assurance people. This is because these problems relate back to issues that occurred during the manufacturing process. Quality assurance personnel are responsible for implementing procedures that prevent these issues from happening, so they are the most logical people to blame.

In reality, problems are always going to occur during manufacturing. People are going to make mistakes even if there are procedures in place to prevent them from doing so because procedures are not 100 percent foolproof. It is not fair to blame quality assurance for problems with finished products, but it does happen and it likely will never completely stop. This is why the "blame game" is a challenge for quality assurance people in manufacturing.

Cutbacks

Quality assurance is a very interesting concept. Many organizational leaders indicate it is one of the most important aspects of manufacturing. However, during tough economic times, it is often one of the first departments where employees are laid off. This is due to the fact that quality assurance personnel are not essential for the physical assembly of products and are therefore expendable when money is tight.

Manufacturers often depend on consistent products, and that consistency is lost when quality assurance departments are eliminated. One might think that this would indicate the importance of quality assurance personnel regardless of the financial situation. However, this is not typically the case...and it the reason why cutbacks are a challenge for quality assurance.

Stress

Quality assurance programs are capable of causing a lot of stress to people within the department. Decisions need to be made that can cause downtime in production, upset people, and make it seem like quality assurance personnel are the "bad guys" who do not care about the well-being of the organization or the people within it.

Leaders of organizations understand that quality assurance people are not out to inflict harm on the organizations that employ them. In fact, their job is to do the exact opposite. They only stop production to make the manufacturing process better in terms of quality and consistency. However, some people's perceptions of quality assurance personnel are negative...and those perceptions are their reality.

Quality assurance personnel want the best for their organizations, but their decisions can slow or halt productivity. They are well aware of their impact of their actions, and the fact that some people will dislike them. Because of this, some quality assurance personnel cannot handle the stress and end up leaving the department.

High expectations

As noted eagerly, continuous improvement means the bar is constantly being raised in terms of quality and consistency. This is great for organizations, but it can be difficult for employees...and quality assurance personnel are charged with the responsibility of making sure those employees rise with the bar.

Additionally, quality assurance people's wages are not always built in to the cost of assembling products. They are tangent to the production process, and this means leadership expects them to perform at high levels in order to justify their wages.

Production training

Manufacturing typically involves a step-by-step process. That process is repeated the same way time after time in order to produce a consistent product. Some processes are simple, while others are quite complicated...and more complex processes require effective employee training.

Unfortunately, many production employees do not get the proper training they need to effectively follow the procedures developed by quality assurance personnel. They do not understand their role in the quality process, and they need to be monitored closely for mistakes and deviations. This is challenging for quality assurance personnel because they must act as "baby sitters" in production situations. It prevents them from concentrating on continuous improvement because their main focus is getting employees to adhere to current standards.

You can now see that quality assurance programs have positives and negatives association with them. Manufacturers that these programs in place need them to perform at the highest levels possible...and that is why improvement is the focus of the next section.

Improving

This section needs to be started with an "absolute must." Quality assurance personnel absolutely must NOT report to production supervisors. If this happens, the whole purpose and function of the quality assurance department are compromised. That being said, any manufacturer that has quality assurance personnel reporting to production management can immediately improve the program by simply changing the organizational hierarchy.

Even if quality assurance does not report to production management, it can be improved. The following are some ways to this:

Draw correlations

The success of quality assurance programs needs to be gauged to assure that they are effective. This is done by measuring customer satisfaction with surveys. The surveys should ask questions about specific areas that were targeted for improvement by quality assurance. For example, if a cell phone manufacturer has procedures in place to make keyboards more sensitive for texting, then a keyboard ease question should be asked.

Results of the surveys should be analyzed to see if there are any correlations between the quality programs implemented and customer satisfaction. If customer satisfaction high, then the quality assurance programs are working and do not need to change. However, if customer satisfaction is low, then changes need to be made.

Change perception

Quality assurance personnel are not the enemy. They are there to help the company, and the changes they make help produce better products that lead to higher sales. That being said, the perception of quality assurance personnel and the procedures they implement needs to change.

This is done by:

> Supplying information
>
>> Like most people, employees do not want to be kept in the dark. They want to know why procedures are in place and who will benefit from them. Skepticism results from a lack of information and quality assurance people are viewed as the reason for it. In short, management needs to inform employees of the reasons why quality assurance personnel do what they do.
>
> Encouraging input
>
>> Sometimes the best way to get information about specific jobs is to ask the people performing those jobs. They know what needs to be done and have often figured out the best way to do it. They might need to change their ways after they give their input, but they will accept the change more readily because they will feel like they were part of the decision making process.

Allow self-evaluation

This is probably the most overlooked method of improvement because it requires an analysis of self rather than others. It is relatively easy for employees to point out the shortcomings of their coworkers, but it is usually much more difficult to pinpoint their own faults. Most employees prefer to point out the positive aspects of their job performance rather than those that are not so positive.

Self-evaluation is another form of employee involvement, but it differs because it asks employees to evaluate their own work in terms of quality. They are given the opportunity to look at the part of the manufacturing process that they control and make suggestions for change. The changes they suggest might be small, but they indicate employees' commitment to the continuous improvement of their organizations.

In short, self-evaluation lets employees feel like they are part of the solution instead of being part of the problem.

Implement training

Proper training prevents problems from occurring. When employees are trained to follow quality assurance procedures, they make fewer mistakes and production lines run more efficiently. This means products can be produced that meet quality, consistency, and cost requirements.

The following are positives that result from employee training in terms of improving quality assurance:

Increased skills

> Organizations want their workers to do their jobs more efficiently and effectively, and this requires up-to-date knowledge and understanding of the tasks they perform. That knowledge and understanding are best obtained using some form of employee training.
>
> The most important part about increased employee skills is the fact that they benefit employees and the organization. Workers benefit by becoming more knowledgeable and valuable in their chosen profession, and organizations benefit by having more competent employees to help meet quality goals and objectives.

Increased motivation

> Motivation is important in any workplace because it drives employees to perform at optimum levels. Without motivation, workers lack the desire to complete job related tasks…and this prevents organizations reaching their potential.
>
> Training allows employees to learn new concepts and better understand the requirements of their jobs. This enables them to work with limited supervision, and the resulting autonomy increases their motivation to make products that meet quality standards.

Increased job satisfaction

> Job satisfaction has been defined in many different ways by a variety of sources. For simplicity purposes, this book views it as employees' like or dislike of their jobs.
>
> Training leads to workers liking their jobs because it provides information that helps them complete assigned tasks. This allows them to experience success…and that success increases their desire to produce quality products.

Increased collaboration

Many employees like to share newly acquired knowledge about their jobs. After all, this knowledge has the greatest value in the workplace because other people are working toward achieving the same goals.

Training provides employees with new knowledge, and that knowledge is shared through collaboration with coworkers. This collaboration encourages workers to think differently due to the diversity of the people involved, and the resulting ideas are beneficial for the overall quality of the organization.

Decreased absenteeism and turnover

Training can be a double-edge sword in terms of turnover. It provides knowledge, and that knowledge can be used to find a better job at another organization. However, this is typically not the case because training inspires loyalty in employees....and that loyalty keeps them working for their current employers. That loyalty also inspires them to emphasize quality in their jobs because they identify with their organizations and the products they produce.

Provide feedback

This suggestion is straightforward and simple. Feedback is essential for improvement of any quality assurance program because employees cannot change if they do not know that they are doing something wrong. They need specific information in order to accomplish the goal of continual improvement, and that information needs to come from quality assurance personnel.

Employees also like to know when they are doing things right. This makes them feel good about their work and encourages them to continue on the same path. It also motivates workers to take ownership of the jobs they perform. When this happens, they need minimal supervision because they know what needs to be done.

In short, feedback is essential for making employees aware of how they are doing in terms of upholding quality standards.

Future

Due to ever increasing customer demands, quality assurance personnel will always be necessary for workplaces. In fact, the functions of quality departments will likely grow as organizations move into the future. That growth, however, will come with changes...so expect the following:

Increased regulatory intervention

A major role of democratic governments is to protect the people that they serve. They work for and are paid by the people of the countries they regulate, and their capacity as overseers continues to grow.

Government officials have their hands in many different aspects of organizational operations, and this shows no signs of tapering off in the future. The United States government, for example, continues to grow in size and increase spending. This allows its employees to expand their roles as overseers of organizations...and quality assurance will fall under their jurisdiction.

Increased customer intervention

Customers want to have a say in the products manufactured for them by their suppliers, especially if those products are private labeled. Two major ways they are doing this include:

Requirements (programs, policies, procedures)

Customers send specific requirements out to the manufacturers of their products. These requirements can dictate processes, specify dimensions, mandate testing, or instruct suppliers to do just about anything else that relates to the quality of the products. If manufacturers refuse to implement these requirements, then they risk losing the business.

Audits

Quality assurance personnel check the actions of production personnel, but who checks the actions of quality assurance personnel? The answer is typically nobody outside of those in top leadership positions...but that is changing, and it will change even more in the future.

Customers will conduct their own audits or contract them out to professional organizations. These audits will assure that specified quality standards are being upheld in addition to the status quo standards that are present in every type of manufacturing.

It is understandable that customers want some control over the products manufactured for them. The extent of that control is debatable, but the fact remains that it is not going to disappear...now or in the future.

Increased technology

Based on what has happened over the past few decades, it is understandable that technology will play a larger role in the quality assurance of manufacturers. This technology will come in the form of software, hardware, and equipment. For example, software will be needed for statistical analysis, hardware will be essential for portable hand-held devices, and equipment will be required for robotics.

Software, hardware, and equipment will become even more important as global competition between manufactures increases. Remote access to all aspects of quality assurance will be required...and that requirement will be met with the advent of new technology.

Increased globalization of standards

Organizations are competing in a world market more than they ever have in the past, and this will not slow down in the future. This is great, but it will have some drawbacks. Many countries have their own standards in terms of quality, and this will need to change if they want to work with each other. There will need to be some type of globalization of quality standards. The exact nature of that globalization is yet to be determined, but it will happen...so expect it!

There is no doubt that standards will change as organizations become global, but the goal for continuous improvement will remain the same. There will always be searches for better standards than those being used. Based on this, it also makes sense that the monitoring of global standards will intensify in the future.

Increased importance on cost

Like it or not, cost is a major concern of manufacturers, and this will not change in the future. This will be bad for quality assurance personnel because their expense is often considered unnecessary for the assembly of products....so they will, therefore, be expendable. Unfortunately, some leaders will never get over the thinking that quality takes a back seat to manufacturing.

However, there is also a positive side to the importance of cost. When quality assurance departments do what they are designed to do, they actually save organizations money by reducing manufacturing errors and customer complaints (see *Cost savings* in the *Advantages* section for details). In other words, quality assurance departments provide a good return on the investment. Therefore, the cost of quality assurance in the future will not be a negative factor...as long the programs function effectively.

Increased emphasis on teamwork

One area of quality assurance that will improve in the future is teamwork. Quality assurance personnel do not always get along with manufacturing employees. Workers in these two departments tend to have different immediate priorities even though their long-term goals are the same. This cannot happen in organizations that have goals of growth and prosperity...and the future will bring about preventative change.

The reduction of conflict between quality assurance and production workers will present some challenges, but it will happen...and the first major step forward will involve empathy training. Employees will learn to understand the difficulties of each other's jobs by "putting themselves in their coworker's shoes." Once they begin to understand each other's roles, the door to teamwork will open wide.

Increased ties to safety

Quality is often tied to safety because regulated processes and procedures prevent employees from making mistakes that could be injurious or deadly. Workers are forced to stay on a proven path because there are consequences for not doing so.

A natural progression for quality assurance is to move into the area of safety management. They understand how to write programs for continual improvement, and the same thinking can be applied to safety in manufacturing plants. This is not necessarily the way it is now, but quality assurance will be involved with safety in the future.

Summary

Quality assurance is important for any manufacturing organization. It ensures that the products produced meet quality and consistency standards so customers will be satisfied. It is a proactive process that benefits organizations in many ways.

This book focuses on quality assurance of products. It describes the topic, discusses its implementation, talks about the advantages and challenges involved, notes methods of improvement, and envisions it in the future. The text is educational and informational, and it is written for easy reader understanding at any level.

Congratulations! You now understand more about quality assurance...an important aspect of any manufacturing organization.

Reference Handbook of Quality in Manufacturing

12 Essential Job Responsibilities

Louis Bevoc and Allison Shearsett

Published by
NutriNiche System LLC

Louis Bevoc books...simple explanations of complex subjects

Introduction — 71
Job responsibilities — 71
- Conformance — 72
- Consistency — 72
- Calibration — 74
- Analysis — 75
- Safety — 75
- Training — 76
- Tracking — 77
- Regulatory — 77
- Validity and reliability — 78
- Functionality — 78
- Application — 79
- Reporting — 79

Summary — 80

Introduction

Some business leaders make quality the most important aspect of their manufacturing processes. They believe quality is the key to taking their organizations to a level above their competition, and they believe people will pay extra money for their products and services because those products and services are worth it. In these leaders' minds, quality is number one...taking priority over everything else.

Quality was first popularized in the United States during the Second World War. It made sure the equipment and supplies manufactured for American troops would perform as expected, and it ended up saving lives. This idea worked well for troops on the battlefield, and after the war, the concept of quality was applied to organizations outside of the military.

Today, quality is a major concern of top managers in most companies. They want people to perceive their businesses as high-end operations that care about their products and services and the customers who purchase them. They believe that the cost of quality is a fraction of the payback, and their organizations' will be the beneficiaries. In the end, defects go down as profitability increases...and this makes stakeholders happy.

Lots of books and articles discuss quality as it relates to business, but few analyze employees in quality departments of production facilities. This book examines quality in manufacturing by exploring the job requirements of quality personnel. Specifically, it focuses on the following 12 job responsibilities:

- Conformance
- Consistency
- Calibration
- Analysis
- Safety
- Training
- Tracking
- Regulatory
- Validity and reliability
- Functionality
- Application
- Reporting

Let's start by defining and discussing the above job responsibilities so they are easily understood by everyone.

Job responsibilities

Job responsibilities are the crux of this book. They provide direction, define skills, designate pay, and create pathways for quality employees to accomplish goals. They also separate quality personnel from the rest of the workforce and provide the basis by which they are judged by their supervisors and coworkers. That being said, 12 specific job responsibilities of quality people in manufacturing are defined and discussed below. The text is written in a simple and easily understandable manner that can be used by readers as a reference at any time. Let's get started.

Conformance

Conformance is the process of getting goods and services to adhere to predetermined criteria. In manufacturing, conformance is the degree to which products meet established standards commonly known as benchmarks. Benchmarks can be standards that need to be met on every production run, such as a box company achieving the same thickness on every corrugated carton, or they can raise the bar with the ultimate goal of continuous improvement, such as a computer manufacturer striving to continually lower defects.

The responsibility for conforming to benchmarks typically falls on the shoulders of quality personnel. They monitor and enforce conformance of products using two somewhat different standards as follows:

Internal standards

Internal standards are those established for the organization, and they are not necessarily the same as external (regulatory or customer) standards. Many times these standards are put in place for cost or yield purposes. For example, a saw manufacturing company might have customer requirement (external standard) that designates blades must have a minimum thickness of .1 inches. However, quality personnel also make sure the blades adhere to an internal standard that prohibits the maximum thickness from exceeding .13 inches. In this instance, quality employees are making sure the saw manufacturer does not "give away" the metal used to make the blades so the company's costs remain in line with the selling price.

External standards

External standards are those established based on regulatory and/or customer requirements. For example, a beverage manufacturer might have a government requirement (external standard) that designates s a plastic bottle must contain at least 2.0 liters of a beverage. In contrast, an internal standard for this bottle might be that it can contain no more than 2.05 liters of beverage to avoid "give away" and maintain product yields for costing purposes. The government requires a minimum beverage volume standard to be in place that must be adhered to by the manufacturer, but the government does not specify a maximum volume standard even though it is enforced by quality personnel via an internal standard.

Regardless of the type of standard, conformance is important in manufacturing because it regulates the products being manufactured. Quality personnel are hired to uphold established standards, and conformance ranks as one of their top job responsibilities.

Consistency

Consistency is similar to conformance, but it refers to making the same product every time rather than meeting standards. For example, assume a chemical manufacturer produces a toilet bowl cleaner that contains bleach. A retail store chain buying this product establishes an external requirement that this product must contain at least five percent bleach. The chemical manufacturer implements an internal standard of no more than five and one-half percent bleach in the toilet bowl cleaner. However, in order to be consistent, the product formulation designates 5.1 percent bleach in every batch. This standard assures that customers will be satisfied and the company will make money, so consistency needs to be monitored by quality personnel.

Another reason for consistency is public perception of the organization. The chemical manufacturer does not want the reputation of being "consistently inconsistent," so they hire quality personnel to watch every batch to assure the amount of bleach added is the same. Consistent products lead to repeat customers because they continually come back to purchase items that they know will perform the same every time they are used.

Unfortunately, consistency is one of the most overlooked aspects of manufacturing, and it is a major reason why quality personnel are in place. Companies want to make the same product time after time, but a wide variety of factors contribute to this not happening. These factors include:

Raw material changes

Raw material can change when manufacturers change suppliers because these new suppliers might not sell the exact same products. An example is a door manufacturing company that decides to buy handles from a new supplier. These handles might not be the same type, design, or composition; thereby jeopardizing the quality of the finished door.

New suppliers are not the only threat to consistency in terms of raw material changes. Current suppliers also present challenges when they decide to make changes regarding their materials, processes, or procedures. For example, a supplier of molds might decide to change their metal to a lower grade of steel; thereby affecting the consistency of the manufacturer's finished product.

Current suppliers also threaten consistency when they short raw materials orders because they force manufacturers to make changes to their formulations or processes. For example, a meat plant might add three percent soy protein to a sausage product, but when their supplier does not completely fill their order, they need to reduce the soy protein added to two percent; thereby affecting the consistency of the finished sausage.

Formulation changes

This refers to formulation changes made by the manufacturer. Formulas are changed for a variety of reasons reduced raw material costs, time savings, improved quality, and better product yields. For example, a bakery might decide to use artificial vanilla instead of the more expensive vanilla extract, so their consistency changes due to lower raw material costs.

The bakery might also decide to save time on their bread manufacturing line by shortening the mixing process. They realize that they can make more bread every shift if they reduce the mixing time of each batch. This increases productivity related aspects of the plant, but it also impacts consistency of the finished loaves of bread.

Regardless of the reason, formulation changes alter product consistency. Customers who do not like these changes react by purchasing similar products from competitors resulting in sales problems for the manufacturer.

Processing changes

Manufacturers can change their processes voluntarily or involuntarily. For example, some managers deliberately change machinery, equipment, or personnel for cost reduction purposes. Their actions are calculated and planned meaning changes in consistency result from intentional decisions.

However, not all actions related to process changes are voluntary. Some changes are forced on manufacturers for reasons beyond their control. Machines become obsolete or parts are no longer able to be ordered, so changes need to be made. The decisions to change are brought about by uncontrollable circumstances, and they affect product consistency.

Regardless of the initial catalyst, processing changes impact product consistency….and the resulting customer complaints cause headaches for manufacturers.

One last important point about consistency is that consistent products are not always good. If a company manufactures a consistently bad product, then consistency has a negative impact on consumer perception. Quality personnel need to understand that this can happen, and their job is to react by suggesting ideas for improvement.

Calibration

Quality personnel are charged with the responsibility of calibrating many different types of equipment in manufacturing facilities. This equipment is found in laboratories, pilot plants, production areas, and even offices. It includes analyzers, meters, scales, thermometers, and other equipment that is needed for manufacturing processes.

Calibration is an important aspect of manufacturing because it makes sure devices used for measuring or analyzing are accurate. The key word is "accurate" because inaccurate measurement creates problems for manufacturers. For example, a scale that is wrongly calibrated will give a false weight every time it is used. If it is a scale used to weight finished products for retail stores, then the customer is never receiving the amount on the package. This problem is compounded for underweight products because the government can issue fines.

Safety is another reason for calibration because inaccurate measurement can injure consumers or make them sick. For example, an uncalibrated food thermometer used to take the temperatures of hot dogs in a meat plant could give a reading higher than the actual temperature; thereby causing consumers who purchase the product to get sick from food borne illness.

One last reason that calibration is needed is certification. Certification is support that products and services meet specific criteria or fall within designated tolerances. For example, a certified paint testing laboratory can assure an elementary school that paint used in the building is lead-free. The laboratory's testing procedure is certified by an official governing body, assuring the school administrators and parents of the children that it is accurate.

In short, calibration prevents errors that can occur in manufacturing facilities. Quality personnel are well aware of the consequences of those errors, and that is a major reason why they are charged with implementing and upholding calibration processes and procedures.

Analysis

Analysis is used in manufacturing to examine something in detail in order to make an interpretation or determination. Often times this involves breaking down or separating individual components for a better understanding. For example, hay is analyzed for moisture to determine if it is ready to sell without the risk of mold or bacterial issues. This analysis involves separating water from the other hay components to determine the moisture content for decision-making purposes.

In terms of job responsibilities, calibration often goes hand-in-hand with analysis for quality personnel. First, they calibrate devices to make sure they are accurate and in proper working order. Then they use the calibrated devices to perform analyses…usually in laboratory settings. For example, a quality person at a dairy calibrates a fat analyzer and then uses it to determine the amount of fat in skim milk.

Statistical process control (SPC) is a specific type of analysis. Essentially, SPC is a form of quality control that collects, interprets, and analyzes data to see if it meets specifications. This type of analysis is employed by quality personnel in a wide variety of manufacturing organizations for problem prevention and continuous improvement.

Analysis is an expected job responsibility of quality personnel in most manufacturing facilities. They need to analyze various aspect of production in order to assure that products and processes are performing as anticipated.

Safety

In terms of safety, quality personnel have a two-fold job responsibility because they need to monitor the safety of employees and consumers; each of which are explained below for a better understanding.

Employees

This refers to the safety of employees. Employee safety involves a lot of rules and regulations depending on the machinery, job, and workplace environment. It can be quite complex, and that is why many organizations have specific people or departments dedicated to making sure employees are safe. However, regardless of the number of people focusing on safety, it is still a responsibility of quality employees. For example, quality personnel often get involved with third party audits that address the safety of employees. There is a fine line between quality and safety job responsibilities, but the personnel from both areas often cross over into each other's territory meaning they need to have a basic understanding of each other's departments.

Quality people also need to inspect equipment and machinery so they need to understand lockout/tagout procedures. Lockout/tagout programs are in place to assure equipment and machines are disconnected from energy sources during any type of service or inspection. This action prevents unexpected energization or startup of machines and equipment; thereby protecting employees from potential harm.

Last, but certainly not least, all quality people are a part of management. Some supervise others, and those who do not are an extension of management. Either way, it is their responsibility to watch out for the safety and well-being of the entire workforce. If a machine is broken or a safety is overridden, quality people need to get involved and report it to the proper authority.

Consumers

This refers to safety of the consumers of the products offered by the employers of quality personnel. Consumers need to be protected from illness and injury, and that protection comes mainly from quality personnel. Quality people implement and uphold policies and procedures that ensure consumer safety. For example, a procedure that protects consumers from injury is a strength test on the chain of a gas powered chain saw. If that chain breaks during usage, it could injure people working with or around it. The fallout from this type of injury could be severe, potentially leaving people maimed for life and/or suing the company for the malfunction.

An example involving illness is quality control personnel at a meat processing plant making sure that ham is cooked to a safe internal temperature. If this product is not cooked to a temperature that kills pathogenic bacteria, then it could make customers sick after they consume it. Technically, this is a job for food safety people, but quality and food safety overlap so it is a quality job responsibility.

Training

Every department in an organization is responsible for some type of training. This training might be formal, such as that in a classroom, or it might be informal, such as watching others do the work during production. Either way, new employees need to be taught the best ways to perform their jobs so they can move beyond the learning curve and start being productive.

Not surprisingly, training is essential in quality departments. However, quality training is different because it is given to employees who are not in the quality department. It is up to quality personnel to show others in their department and outside of their department how to do things correctly. For example, nut and bolt manufacturing employees need to be taught how to perform their jobs within specific tolerances. Quality personnel show employees what they need to do in order to meet those tolerances. This might seem like it is a direct responsibility of production supervisors, but that is typically not the case. Production supervisors specify the number of nuts and bolts that need to be manufactured and the order in which they need to be completed. Quality oversight is a direct job responsibility of quality personnel.

Quality training in manufacturing takes place at two points in the process. First, new hires are shown how to do their jobs properly so they do not start out on the wrong foot. This is important because once employees do something wrong, it is difficult to change their mindset to the right way of doing things. Often times quality personnel are not the primary trainers of new hires, but they need to be present to oversee the process when other production workers do the training.

Once the production new hires understand their jobs, they can be trained on more detailed quality aspects by quality personnel. This can involve on-the-job training or classroom learning. On-the-job training works well for showing exactly what needs to be done while classroom training allows for focus on the overall quality process. Either way, employees need to do their jobs with quality in mind, and training is the best way put them in the proper mindset.

Tracking

Tracking is an important job responsibility of quality personnel because it is critical for establishing the trends necessary for problem isolation and resolution. Without proper tracking, manufacturers are not able to see where they are making mistakes; thereby preventing them from taking the action necessary to correct those mistakes. For example, a bakery is experiencing a problem because their bread is not properly rising. They need to track all ingredients used in the production of their bread so they have the ability to look for reasons why their bread is not rising as specified. The company might have switched brands or types of yeast, and this problem can be identified using a trend found with tracking.

Tracking also indicates customer complaints that need to be addressed. If the bakery has one complaint on the taste of their blueberry pies, then this does not indicate a trend and no action is required. However, if they have multiple taste complaints on these pies, then the trend indicates some type of action must be taken to prevent the loss of sales.

Surveys are a form of tracking that can help prevent sales losses. Quality personnel are often responsible for issuing customer satisfaction surveys and using the results to look for trends. These trends can be positive, such as people liking a new croissant, or they can be negative, such as people disliking the size of a roll. Either way, the information gathered is useful and quality personnel are responsible for obtaining it.

Regulatory

Quality people in most manufacturing plants are responsible for the upholding the regulations that must be followed by their employers. They deal directly with the government agencies that oversee those regulations, sometimes even getting to know the employees of those agencies by name. Examples include quality personnel in food processing plants. They interact on a daily basis with USDA inspectors and form relationships with those individuals. This relationship can be helpful in difficult situations, but it must always be remembered that USDA inspectors are paid to make sure plants are in compliance with rules regulations....not to be the friends of those employed in the quality departments.

People who have worked in quality positions understand the importance of their regulatory roles. They know they can prevent disaster from occurring by making sure their organizations follow government mandated rules and regulations. Unfortunately, their coworkers do not always understand this importance...until their work is stopped by government agencies due to regulatory violations. An example is a pharmaceutical manufacturer that has their production halted by FDA (Food and Drug Administration) officials due to less than sterile conditions. Production employees cannot work and are subsequently sent home until the proper action is taken to comply with the regulations by making the production area sterile.

One additional comment about quality people and regulatory responsibility is their need to be honest and ethical. Lying, falsifying documents, or hiding the facts are unacceptable because these deceptions paint an untrue picture of organizations. More importantly, discovery of these illegal or unethical activities by government personnel can result in a plant management getting in more trouble than they would have if quality people told the truth. In terms of quality personnel and regulatory responsibilities, it is always best to remember the old saying, "Oh what a web we weave, when we practice to deceive."

Validity and reliability

This is the extent to which something is accurate in the present circumstances. In other words, it tells whether something measures what it is supposed to measure. For example, if a detergent manufacturing plant wants to weigh an ingredient for formulations purposes, it must use a valid and reliable scale to obtain that weight. Quality personnel have the responsibly of making sure that the proper scale is chosen for the job. They need a scale that measures to 1/10th of a pound and cannot use a scale that rounds up or down to the nearest pound in order meet the formulation requirements. Additionally, they need to make sure the chosen scale is calibrated by testing it with certified weights. This assures the scale measurement will be the same time after time. If the correct sale is used and it is properly calibrated, then it is valid and reliable because it is measuring what it is supposed to measure on a consistent basis.

Validity is important for many different aspects of manufacturing. Weights and measures are common examples, but it also has value for temperature, humidity, pH, color, density, composition, and time. For example, a steel manufacturer that needs to forge metal at a specific temperature needs an accurate thermometer for measurement. Along the same lines, an electronics manufacturer in Southern California needs accurate measurement of humidity to assure their finished products will work as designed in humid climates such as Florida and Mississippi. They need to create environments that mimic the humid conditions of the deep-south which means the validity of the humidity measuring instrument is critical. Quality personnel are charged with the responsibility of making sure that instrument is accurate and reliable.

Functionality

Quality personnel have the responsibly of checking finished products for functionality. This responsibility takes place in the manufacturing plant after products roll off the line and are ready to be released for sale. It is the final in plant check done to indicate whether or not products work as designed.

These checks are often very simple and do not involve any type of equipment or machinery. A visual analysis is sometimes enough to make a determination. For example, a paint manufacturing quality person might simply look at the color and consistency as it is deposited in into the container to confirm it looks right. Her experience is enough for her to know that the product looks right as it goes through the final process. Other functional checks can go beyond a visual analysis and still be quite simple. For example, a quality person in an electric fan manufacturer facility might remove a fan from the line and plug it into to an electrical outlet. If the fan turns on and appears to work properly, then it is functional.

In many ways, functionality is the most basic quality responsibility. Functional products are expected by everyone, and it is assumed that they will be checked before being released for sale to consumers.

Application

This is an interesting quality responsibility that differs from functionality because it takes place in the hands of the consumers rather than in a laboratory or manufacturing facility. Many products work during the research and development stages, and they also do fine plant settings. However, this success is not transferred when these products are shipped out to customers. When this happens, complaints start to mount, returns are inevitable and repeat customers diminish. For these reasons, application to real world settings is critical...and quality personnel are charged with this responsibility. This requires going past the testing and production phases by getting products into the hands of customers. It is a rather simple process, but it can be overlooked, especially if everyone involved thinks the product is a sure bet for market success.

Probably the most famous failure of application came in 1985 when Coca-Cola introduced its newly formulate flagship item, known worldwide as Coke. Their secret century-old formula was changed without fully testing its effects on real world customers resulting in chaos and public outcry. People started hoarding the old Coke, and this prompted a return of Coca-Cola classic.

Obviously, quality personnel are not fully responsible for the Coca-Cola blunder. It was a major marketing mistake and decisions were made by executives much higher up the corporate ladder. However, quality was a concern with this debacle, and Coke's quality personnel shared in the blame. If they had been a little more aggressive and vocal when testing the new formula in the real world, then they could have potentially averted the disaster.

Essentially, many different people in organizations have application responsibilities. A group effort is needed to assure people will accept new products put on the market by manufacturers. However, this responsibility is one the many shouldered by quality personnel, and that is why it is mentioned in this handbook.

Reporting

In some manufacturing plants, reporting is the biggest and most important job responsibility of quality employees because it provides management with information that allows them to introduce new products, make changes to existing products, or eliminate products that are not well-received by customers. This reporting can be done at any phase of the manufacturing process, including follow-up after the product has been released for sale.

Pre-shipment reporting is done before or during manufacturing, and it often involves the collection of data for analysis. An example is a report on the strength of a jump rope after it has been put through multiple stress tests. Data can also be collected to show the number of nonconformances experienced during production. An example is a percentage based on the number of incidents that a screw has to be scrapped because it not properly threaded.

Other reporting comes after the product is released for sale. Again data is collected, but that data comes from customer reactions to the products they have purchased. An example is the results of a survey used to determine customer acceptance of a new cell phone. As mentioned earlier, surveys are part of the tracking responsibility of quality people, but they also entail a reporting responsibility.

Reporting provides useful information that can be used by many different employees in organizations. Research and development people apply it to future projects so they do not repeat the same mistakes, sales and marketing people get a better idea of the customers' perception of quality, accountants use it for determining impact on the bottom line, and quality people use it for continuous improvement. It is an important aspect of manufacturing that is at the forefront of quality people's responsibilities.

Summary

This book is a reference for 12 important job responsibilities of quality personnel in manufacturing. It breaks down each responsibility into simple terms and discusses its importance. The following job responsibilities are included:

- Conformance
- Consistency
- Calibration
- Analysis
- Safety
- Training
- Tracking
- Regulatory
- Validity and reliability
- Functionality
- Application
- Reporting

The above job responsibilities will expand as manufacturing leaders realize the value of quality for making the best possible products in the face of global competition.

Congratulations! You now understand more about jobs responsibilities of quality personnel in manufacturing....and this book can be used as a reference whenever it is needed.

Made in the USA
Lexington, KY
30 May 2019